Good Guys with Guns

GOOD GUYS
WITH GUNS

Alan Gottlieb

&

Dave Workman

Merril Press
Bellevue, WA 98005

GOOD GUYS WITH GUNS
is published by
Merril Press, P.O. Box 1682, Bellevue, WA 98009.
www.merrilpress.com
Phone: 425-454-7009
Distributed to the book trade by
Independent Publishers Group (IPG)
814 N. Franklin Street, Chicago, IL 60610
www.ipg.com
Trade Order Placement: 1-800-888-4741

FIRST EDITION

Library of Congress Cataloging-in-Publication Data

ISBN 978-0-936783-69-7

Printed in the United States of America

DEDICATION

To the hundreds of thousands of law-abiding firearms owners who have used firearms to defend themselves and their loved ones, and the thousands of instructors who taught them, and to The Founders, who understood that the right to Bear arms is the right to Carry them.

Table of Contents

FOREWORD

Whether they are referred to as "armed private citizens," "self-defense advocates" or "gun-toting Samaritans," legally-armed Americans are now widely identified as "Good Guys with Guns."

Throughout the history of this country, dating back to colonial days, through the period of westward exploration and expansion—including but not limited to the "Wild West" era that made heroes of such men as James Butler "Wild Bill" Hickok, William F. "Buffalo Bill" Cody, Bat Masterson, Wyatt Earp, Luke Short and even the likes of Jesse James, Cole Younger and William "Billy the Kid" Bonney—up through the *Gay Nineties*, *Roaring Twenties* and into modern times, there have been quiet, peaceful citizens who kept and relied upon firearms for personal and family protection and subsistence.

They were self-reliant, occasionally the only semblance of law (with or without order), and ultimately the masters of their own fate. These nameless good citizens occasionally rode in posses, chased rustlers, fought back against night riders in the post-Civil War South and on at least two notable occasions—Sept. 7, 1876 in Northfield, Minnesota and Oct. 5, 1892 in Coffeyville, Kansas—provided reinforcements to town lawmen to shoot the James-Younger and Dalton gangs, respectively, thus bringing an end to those notorious outlaw gangs.

In more modern times, armed citizens have stepped forward, occasionally at great peril, to defend their communities. Many armed citizens opened fire on Texas Tower sniper Charles Whitman to keep him pinned down while police officers and one private citizen made their way to the top of the building to stop the mass killer who had killed 16 people and wounded many others.

None of these citizens ever intended to find themselves in the middle of gun battles. They were ordinary people who were suddenly faced with extraordinary circumstances.

More typically, armed citizens act in self-defense against one or more criminals. They may be convenience store clerks, pharmacists, neighbors and friends, and occasionally total strangers who step in at a critical moment to save the life of another. This book includes anecdotal stories of armed citizens who intervened to save the lives of police officers, and others who drew legally-carried defensive sidearms to prevent mass shootings.

The very last place any of these brave citizens ever wanted to be was in the middle of a gunfight. Yet in every situation, they became the proverbial "first responder" because—as the saying goes—when seconds count, the police are minutes away.

This phenomenon of armed citizens defending themselves and others is not uniquely American, but it is close. The United States does stand apart from other nations thanks to the Second Amendment, which protects, rather than grants, the right to keep and bear arms. It is a great misunderstanding that any part of the Constitution gives us anything. The Bill of Rights protects preexisting natural and human rights, frequently called "God-given rights" and the oldest of these is the natural right of self-preservation.

Our Founding Fathers were pretty smart guys; visionaries well ahead of their times who had just gone through a bloody revolution, defeating the most powerful military force on the planet at the time. They created a Republic and endeavored to protect the rights of all citizens to defend and preserve that nation.

The volunteers who formed early militias in the Mohawk Valley, stood shoulder-to-shoulder on Lexington Commons and Concord Bridge, who fought British Regulars from Breeds and Bunker Hills to Yorktown, they were also "good guys with guns." They laid the groundwork upon which the nation was built.

Times, of course, have changed. But the right of self-preservation is as clear and sacred today as it has always been. History has provided many bandits, highwaymen and outlaws, and there are still such criminals on the landscape today. That's why the notion of private citizens being armed has never really become passé.

The first time we tackled this subject was in *America Fights Back: Armed Self-Defense in a Violent Age*. While this book might be considered a sequel, it will also stand on its own as a testament to the times in which we live, because defending one's self, family and home should never fall out of style.

By some estimates, as this book was written, some 17 million private citizens across the 50 states are legally licensed to carry concealed sidearms. There is a smaller but dedicated movement of citizens who still openly carry handguns, which is legal in many states. As the number of armed citizens continues to expand, the odds increase exponentially that there will be confrontations pitting good against evil, usually much to the surprise of the bad guys. While they may or may not set out to harm anyone while they commit crimes, they absolutely *never* expect to get shot, and sometimes killed, as a result of their illegal behavior.

The would-be rapist who suddenly finds himself staring into the muzzle of a legally-carried handgun held by his intended victim, or the thug who enters a convenience store with a stolen gun only to be confronted by a graveyard shift manager with a legally-owned pistol are the types of people who keep the Second Amendment relevant in the 21st Century.

The single woman who attends a self-defense course, the father who works a second job at night to provide for his young family, the retiree who made it this far and wants to enjoy those "golden years" understand that their lives have value. They are not about to lose everything they have to some thief in the night or some maniac with a grudge, so they quietly join the ranks of armed citizens, hoping they never have to use their firearms for serious business, same as they pay insurance premiums on home and car, hoping they never have to call the insurance agent.

Whether the gun prohibition and anti-self-defense lobbying groups want to admit it, the armed private citizen is the backbone of their neighborhood. Their mere presence in the community sometimes provides an unseen layer of protection from petty would-be criminals who might avoid some place or neighborhood for fear of encountering an armed citizen.

There have been anecdotal situations in which crime drops, even if only temporarily, in an area where some miscreant has met an untimely demise at the hands of a man or woman who had the will and the way to fight back. No criminal hoping to become a recidivist is going to press his luck by knowingly trying to victimize someone who just might shoot him dead.

"Good Guys with Guns" is not just a catch phrase designed to attract attention. It refers to a genuine, and perhaps even special, group of men and women who have realized that they are ultimately responsible for their own well-being, and perhaps the safety of family and friends in their presence.

They are the people who stand apart from the crowd. They are the ones who, in a country often described as a "nation of sheep," are not part of the flock. They are the sheep dogs who help keep the wolves and coyotes at bay.

Sincerely—Alan Gottlieb and Dave Workman

1: THE GOOD GUYS HAVE HAD ENOUGH

Apparently, the gun-wielding attacker who strolled into an Oklahoma City restaurant one evening and began shooting randomly at the people inside didn't get the memo that Americans have had enough.

When he opened fire at the popular Louie's Grill & Bar, probably the last thing he expected to encounter was the last thing he actually did encounter: not one but two legally-armed private citizens identified as Carlos Nazario and Bryan Wittle. In a matter of seconds, would-be mass shooter Alexander C. Tilghman of Oklahoma City was down and permanently out, fatally-wounded in a mass shooting gone bad, or perhaps good, depending upon one's perspective.

As CNN and other news agencies reported the incident, it became clear that "good guys with guns" had won…again. It wasn't the first time, and it definitely wasn't the last time, as events since that deadly confrontation have demonstrated. It is happening with a bit more frequency as increasing numbers of citizens are going armed. They have taken to heart a sarcasm that has made the rounds repeatedly within the shooting community: "When seconds count, police are minutes away."

Legally-armed private citizens have become the first responders in a number of incidents, publicized more in recent times because it is something of a recent phenomenon. The "good guy with a gun" story now seems to appeal more to news agencies. It is more than just a decision that "if it bleeds, it leads." The idea of average citizens doing something heroic, something that a quarter-century ago might have been unheard of across much of the United States, is a concept that enjoys growing popularity.

There was no indication that Tilghman, the attacker in Oklahoma City, was some sort of fanatic, but he has joined a number of others in the historical dust bin that contains the names and other vital statistics of people who made terminally wrong choices. By all accounts, he entered the popular restaurant wearing ear and eye protection as though he were entering a gun range and started shooting with no known motive. There did not appear to be any history of mental illness, and he did not apparently know anyone at the restaurant.

Nazario and Wittle, who did not know one another, both quickly retrieved handguns from their vehicles.

There is a lesson in this tale. If your twisted plan is to open fire at a crowded theater, big box store, restaurant, shopping mall or some other public place, the odds are gradually increasing that waiting for you somewhere in that crowd of would-be victims is someone to stop you.

According to research conducted by Pew Research, 48 percent of the people who own firearms bought them for personal protection. Whether they actually ever use those guns in an act of self-defense is debatable, but the trend appears to be gradually increasing. NPR reported that a Harvard University analysis – using data from the National Crime Victimization Survey – suggests that the use of firearms in self-defense remains a rare event. The Harvard report indicated that armed citizens defended themselves with firearms in only 0.9 percent of crimes committed from 2007 through 2011.

Former Congresswoman Gabrielle "Gabby" Giffords, who survived an assassination attempt at a Tucson, Arizona shopping center and is now a leading national gun control advocate, relied on that NPR report to declare in a post on Twitter, that the "good guy with a gun narrative is a myth meant to scare people into buying guns for self-defense."

However, Giffords' assertion may have a credibility problem of its own. The annual FBI Uniform Crime Report reveals that between the years 2012 and 2017, the most recent year for which data was available at this writing, armed private citizens killed more than 1,500 attackers during the commission of a felony. In most of those instances, the armed citizens used handguns, while rifles or shotguns accounted for a fraction of the self-defense shootings (just as long guns account for a fraction of homicides, somewhere in the 2-3 percent range in any given year).

These incidents are investigated carefully by local law enforcement agencies. It is up to detectives from those agencies to consider all the facts, take statements from the people who fired those fatal shots, and present all of that information to prosecutors who then balance it all against their individual state's self-defense and/or use-of-force statutes.

There are times when these incidents get more than just local media attention. In the case of the Oklahoma City shooting, it landed in the national spotlight because, even today with more than 17 million legally-licensed Americans carrying firearms for personal and family protection, "community defense" shootings in which armed citizens shoot and/or kill somebody engaged in a criminal act are rare.

Two of those rare events happened in Washington State. In one case, an armed citizen was enjoying a morning cup of coffee at a convenience store near his home in the Seattle area when a man later identified as Steven Blacktongue, then 43, rushed through the doorway and immediately began swinging a large hatchet. He barely missed the armed citizen with one horrendous swing that might have, if he connected, decapitated the citizen.

The event was captured on the store's security video system, and it showed everything from the first swing to the moment Blacktongue went down, having been shot three times at virtually point-blank range by the Samaritan, who was armed that morning with a pair of Smith & Wesson double-action revolvers in .357 Magnum caliber, one in each pocket of his jacket.

At close range, a 125-grain bullet fired from even a short-barreled .357 Magnum revolver will leave the muzzle traveling at about 1,200 feet-per-second. It will slam into whatever it hits with the energy of a sledgehammer, and in this case, the man who had mounted the unprovoked attack collapsed into a heap, expiring a few moments later.

The armed citizen, who has preferred to maintain his anonymity in this case, had never served in the military or as a civilian peace officer, but he was an experienced gun owner. A member of the Washington Arms Collectors, he frequently visited the convenience store to visit with the proprietor or one of the staff, with whom he was acquainted, and enjoy a cup of coffee.

It was not known why Blacktongue, who had a history of substance abuse, attacked. But it was his last act, and as the armed citizen subsequently observed, Blacktongue called the play, nobody else.

King County Sheriff's investigators showed up within minutes, but as is typical, they arrived just in time to start diagramming the crime scene. They didn't fire a shot.

After a lengthy interview, and after detectives carefully reviewed the security video, they released the armed citizen and no charges were ever filed. After about 90 days, the citizen's handgun was returned. He later confided to one of the authors that some deputies were "impressed" that he routinely carries two guns instead of just one. And, he added, he has never endured a sleepless night over the incident. This armed citizen did what had to be done, and he has no regrets.

But a now-retired King County Sheriff's sergeant summed it up at the time with this perspective: "Fortunately, because of this customer with his weapon, this could have been a lot worse. The clerk could be the one laying there dead on the floor right now."

More than two years after that incident, and two counties away, an armed citizen fatally shot a crazed man who had been involved in three attempted carjackings, fired shots inside a Walmart, then went outside where he attempted to hijack another car, shooting the driver twice in the process.

In this incident, at least two armed citizens moved in to stop the mayhem. One of those men was David George, a pastor at a church in a neighboring county who was shopping on Father's Day with his family. An

EMT and volunteer fireman in his community, George has also had training in self-defense and active shooter scenarios. When he had a clear shot, he fired.

The dead man, 42-year-old Tim Day, had recently lost a job, according to various reports, but that did not adequately explain his wild behavior.

Under Washington statute dating back decades, homicide by a private citizen is justifiable in self-defense or the defense of another innocent person. Pastor George was acting not only in his defense, but out of concern for his family, and because he had just witnessed a series of events including the shooting of a motorist that would have convinced any reasonable person that intervention was necessary to prevent any further violence. In a parking lot outside a major retail store, that potential was at 100 percent.

In both Washington State cases, and the Oklahoma City case, public reaction was swift. The armed citizens were considered heroes for placing themselves in harm's way to protect other people. In the case of Pastor George, after he shot Day, he asked fellow armed citizen Jesse Zamora to keep the fatally wounded man covered while he, George, grabbed his First Aid bag and began treating the seriously wounded motorist, Ricky Fievez, who was left paralyzed by one of the two bullets that Day fired into him.

'Good Guy with a gun'

Following the horrible tragedy at Sandy Hook Elementary in Newtown, Connecticut in 2012, the National Rifle Association made headlines when it issued a statement several days after the shooting that boiled down to this: "The only thing that stops a bad guy with a gun is a good guy with a gun."

This was a matter-of-fact, sound bite statement essentially designed to underscore the recommendation that school districts consider various options including armed security guards on every school campus in the country.

In the aftermath of that appearance, a hostile national media excoriated the pro rights organization for making the argument, but in the months that followed, the hypocrisy of the establishment became clear. Several school districts around the country began quietly doing exactly what had been suggested. They just didn't give any credit to the organization for broaching the subject. Indeed, in most cases it was as though the idea had begun with local school administrators.

In many schools, members of the teaching staff or administrators took special training and began very covertly carrying firearms on school grounds.

In other cases, schools hired off-duty police officers or sheriff's deputies, and in still other cases, local law enforcement agencies began assigning "school resource officers" to be on campuses, or patrol in certain neighborhoods where schools are located to reduce their response time to an emergency call.

Nobody wanted, or dared, to give credit to a pro-rights organization for planting the seed that grew into what now appears to be a widely-accepted program. But all of it followed Sandy Hook, and all of it was essentially an outgrowth of the organization's statement.

In the years since that tragic event, there have been incidents at schools in Maryland, Colorado and elsewhere that found a school resource officer engaging an active shooter. The "good guy with a gun" doesn't have to be a policeman or an armed private citizen. He, or she, only needs to be the "good guy" and have a gun. Nothing could be more simple to understand. Meet force with force to stop the threat.

Incredibly, there remain individuals and organizations that are fundamentally opposed to the concept of defending the defenseless by the use of force. Even when there is absolutely no conceivable doubt that the criminal who takes a bullet has it coming, self-defense opponents seem to emerge from the woodwork to decry what has occurred.

Fortunately, America seems to be in the process of a cultural shift in that regard. It may take years, perhaps a couple of generations, but as noted earlier, the "good guys" have had enough. For them, it's a realization that America tried a grand experiment of leniency and rehabilitation and reducing violence through non-violent methods and for the criminal element has been an abject failure.

Gun control laws, for example, have primarily affected those citizens who would never consider breaking the law to begin with. History has taught us that any criminal with evil intentions will find a way to get his or her hands on a firearm, even if it involves stealing it from a police officer.

Bad guys don't even need firearms. They've discovered cars and trucks as weapons of mass destruction, as illustrated by attacks in Toronto and New York.

Such incidents have reminded average citizens that violence does not occur on a prearranged schedule, and criminals or crazy people determined to harm innocent people do not call ahead and make an appointment. So, this notion of a private citizen thrust by circumstances beyond his or her control to become a "first responder" is gradually being accepted by the public, especially if such a hero saves them from harm.

Average citizens, extraordinary circumstances

What is a "hero?" In the case of armed citizens who respond to violent events, they are typically average citizens suddenly faced with extraordinary circumstances. They come in all sizes and shapes; there is no exclusivity of race or creed. Age doesn't seem to be a factor.

The only thing they all have in common is that they are armed. Despite years of political attempts to erode their right to bear arms, these good guys (and gals) with guns have gone through the effort to obtain carry permits or licenses, allowing them to possess defensive sidearms so they are prepared to defend themselves and others. Many go through training from simple beginner's courses to advanced classes, and they are quite often skilled marksmen and women.

Following the Oklahoma City incident, one police captain told reporters, "These guys were protecting somebody else's life. You can say they are heroes."

But "good guys with guns" are typically quiet about their deeds. Many shy completely away from publicity. Others have it thrust upon them whether they like it or not.

Stephen Willeford, the soft-spoken Texas man who intervened in a mass shooting at the church across the street from his home in Sutherland Springs, did an Op-Ed column for the *Dallas Morning News* in which he observed, "Anti-gun politicians and anti-gun activists have made clear their belief that the way to stop criminals is to restrict the rights of law-abiding citizens, and many have blamed the men and women of the NRA for acts of deranged individuals. Sometimes, it feels like the mainstream media hates firearms.

"I am proof that they (anti-gunners) are wrong," he continued. "I am also proof that the NRA's familiar mantra is true: The best way to stop a bad guy with a gun is a good guy with a gun."

Willeford shot the church gunman when he emerged from the building. The killer was armed with a so-called "assault weapon," an AR-15 type rifle. Coincidentally, so was Willeford. He had run to retrieve the rifle and load it as he rushed to confront the shooter. It was no surprise that this fact was widely played down by media reports; the fact that a private citizen used a firearm that the press routinely demonizes, to shoot a mass killer and cause him to flee the crime scene does not play well with what appears to be an anti-gun narrative.

It was mass killer Devin Kelley's bad luck that Willeford is also a certified firearms instructor, and therefore a fairly skilled marksman. Kelley was someone who should not have had a firearm, due to his criminal convictions during his military service. That information, for some reason, was apparently not provided to the National Instant Check System (NICS) that is operated by the FBI. Thus, Kelley was able to purchase firearms while residing in Colorado and Texas without being flagged as disqualified.

Willeford wrote in the Op-ed article that, "when my daughter told me there was a shooter and I heard the shots myself, I fell back on my years of NRA training, grabbed my AR-15, and ran across the street to engage the shooter. People say I saved lives that day. I hope that's true. I did what the Lord called me to do."

He added, "We are not the bad guys."

Right; Willeford and other law-abiding American gun owners are the good guys. More often than not, these legally-armed citizens are the biggest and most unwelcome surprise that criminals or crazies encounter, and as noted earlier it is frequently the last surprise of their lives.

An incident that occurred in DeKalb County, Georgia was just such a situation. According to the report at WSB-TV, three would-be robbers ended up in the hospital after they made a massive error in the victim selection process. The trio were in a store and apparently followed two people outside to the parking lot.

What ensued was chaotic, according to various published reports. The three bad guys were armed, but so was one of the intended victims, who they were either trying to rob or carjack. When the shooting was over, all three suspects were injured. They were charged with assorted crimes. Considering that a lot of criminals are killed by the people they're trying to victimize, this bunch might have been lucky.

No Shots Fired

As is frequently the case, an armed citizen doesn't need to actually fire a shot to bring a confrontation to an end. While the gun control lobby has labored to diminish the importance of armed self-defense, citing the aforementioned FBI data that only reports actual self-defense killings and not the large number of situations in which nobody is killed, or even shot.

That point was made rather bluntly by *National Review's* Kevin D. Williamson, writing that the argument is "dumb to the point of intellectual dishonesty" because not all defensive firearms uses involve the killing of another person.

Indeed, Williamson observed, "Nobody but nobody is quite so dumb as to believe that all, most, or even very many uses of firearms to prevent acts of criminal violence result in justifiable homicides. Most of them do not result in any body being shot, much less shot dead, because most of them do not involve discharging a firearm. As it turns out, pointing a gun at a would-be assailant is in many cases a very persuasive gesture."

One such case occurred in Florida, where a woman identified by Fox News as Lauren Richards was forced by circumstances to confront an intruder and hold him at gunpoint for an incredible 25 minutes while waiting for police to arrive. This is one of those "when seconds count" situations mentioned earlier. In some rural parts of the country, police or sheriff's deputies might not show up for an hour or more, or not at all.

According to the published account, the 25-year-old Richards lived in the Tampa Bay area. She dialed 911 just after midnight on the night in question, telling the call receiver that a stranger was lurking outside of her home. According to the report, originally filed by WFLA, Richards noticed that her garage door was closed when it was normally kept open. She opened the door and found the man about eight feet away.

After about ten minutes following her first 911 call, no police appeared so she called a second time to tell the call receiver that she had the suspect at gunpoint and needed help immediately. It was another 13 minutes, according to WFLA, before police finally did arrive. In the meantime, a neighbor did appear to assist Richards in holding the suspect at gunpoint, but only after she called him.

Richards is a mother with small children. In a similar situation, what would any reasonable person do, and what might they think about police response time?

Out west in Phoenix, Arizona, an armed citizen intervened one morning when a man reportedly tried to kidnap an 11-year-old girl who was on her way to school. According to the local Fox News affiliate, the armed Samaritan spotted the suspect and confronted him, knocking him down and then aimed his handgun at the suspect.

At that point, the suspect fled, but police did have a description and a photo of the suspect.

Up in Seattle, Washington, a "good Samaritan with a concealed carry permit" was credited with "helping to subdue" a murder suspect who had moments before fatally stabbed a woman in the Food Court area of the Seattle Center. The whole incident was captured on video from at least two perspectives by different witnesses, and the hero in this case, identified as Scott Brown, could easily have shot the suspect, later identified as David Lee Morris.

According to published reports, Morris admitted that he stabbed Gabrielle Garcia, with whom he had a 5-year-old son, in a domestic dispute. She had filed a protection order against him, a fact that should underscore the ineffectiveness of a piece of paper in a life-or-death situation.

As he walked away from the stabbing scene, Morris was confronted by Brown, who had drawn his legally-carried sidearm. For the next several tense minutes, Brown held Morris at gunpoint as the suspect reportedly begged to be shot.

A second citizen approached the suspect and pepper-sprayed him. Moments later Seattle police arrived and took Morris into custody, according to KCPQ, the local Fox affiliate.

A legally-armed Florida resident held a 14-year-old suspect at gunpoint after the youth reportedly threatened a female customer in the aisle of a Walmart, demanding sex. The teen was armed with a knife, which is typically no match for a gun in such a confrontation.

According to a published report, the armed citizen responded to the woman's cry for help, drew his gun and held him for responding sheriff's deputies. That lad was hauled away for a mental evaluation, which was considerably less deadly than what could have occurred.

'Active Shooter Incidents'

The FBI published an interesting 18-page document called "Active Shooter Incidents in the United States in 2016 and 2017." The "mass" shooting has become a news staple, and during those two years in 21 states, there were 50 such incidents, according to the FBI report.

In those 50 incidents, there were 943 casualties, including 221 killed and 723 wounded. Among those killed were 13 police officers, and 20 more were among the wounded. Fourteen of those incidents ended with an exchange of gunfire between the bad guys and police.

Of the 50 shooters, all were men. An incident in 2018 involving a woman who opened fire at a tech establishment in California was a rarity.

Among the shooters, 13 committed suicide, 11 were killed by police and eight were stopped by private citizens. Eighteen more were apprehended by police.

An increasing number of businesses and public schools are now training for "active shooter" scenarios. As noted earlier in this chapter, many schools now have armed security of some form or another, and many businesses are also providing employee training.

As anecdotal information about active shooter incidents, coupled with local crime reports in communities across the nation, is it any wonder that millions of citizens have decided to arm themselves? There essentially is an army of "good guys with guns" and it is expanding, though not nearly as much as it might have grown had the 2016 presidential and congressional elections turned out differently.

An incidental side effect of having gun control proponents in the White House and on Capitol Hill is that increasing numbers of Americans buy guns and obtain carry licenses. It is part of the equation of public concern – call it fear – that government is going to ratchet down on the right to keep and bear arms, so Americans act in advance of such an eventuality.

That must be considered a small manifestation of the overall movement toward "arming up." The primary reason people have guns, according to various surveys, is for personal protection. Other reasons, including hunting, target shooting, recreation, competition or collecting trail behind self-defense.

Self-preservation is the oldest natural right. In America, where bad guys routinely ignore every law and morality is never a consideration, good guys increasingly want to level the playing field. For decades, thanks to strict gun control policies, this was not possible in many jurisdictions. But over the years as gun laws were reformed to allow more citizens to exercise their constitutional rights, that situation has obviously changed.

The Colorado Confrontation

Several months after the mass shooting at the church in Sutherland Springs, and a couple of states away, another man armed with an AR-15 semi-automatic rifle stopped a gunman who, according to KUSA News, had been firing shots at passing cars on a highway in Colorado's Douglas County.

It was the gunman's bad luck that during his shooting spree, he encountered retired Alabama lawman Wesley Mattox, who happened to be camping with his wife in the Pike National Forest on a pleasant July day.

The incident began when the suspect carjacked a Mazda hatchback in El Paso County and began firing at people. At some point, the stolen car suffered a flat tire, but that didn't stop the gunman from continuing his rampage.

Published reports say the gunman finally made his way to a campsite in the Devil's Head Campground, where the confrontation with Mattox began. The carjacker pulled up, and began yelling. The 51-year-old

Mattox approached the Mazda to determine what the problem was, and the suspect aimed a rifle at him and demanded water.

Mattox beat a hasty retreat to his camp and armed himself with his own semi-auto rifle, retrieved from his truck and camper. That was after he armed his wife with a handgun and told her to take cover.

The "good guy with a gun" moved away from the camper to draw fire away from where his wife was huddled, and opened fire after telling the suspect to drop his gun and getting shot at for his effort.

Now, here's where the story gets very interesting. When Mattox believed he had run out of ammunition, he raced back to his truck and retrieved a second AR-15 rifle to continue the battle! He fired one more round at the suspect, who had crashed his stolen car into a tree.

By the time that happened, Mattox had shot the gunman, who survived and was charged with numerous crimes.

The great lesson in the Colorado case is the same lesson that could be learned from any number of other life-threatening incidents in which an armed citizen becomes the first responder: Violence happens pretty much by surprise, and like the Boy Scouts have taught generations of youth, "always be prepared."

And that brings us back around to the premise that "good guys with guns" can stop bad guys, and have done so repeatedly.

Keep in mind that Mattox, like Texan Stephen Willeford and Oklahomans Carlos Nazario and Bryan Wittle were ordinary citizens in the process of minding their own business and living routine lives when they were suddenly thrust into extraordinary circumstances beyond their control. That has actually been how some people describe heroes.

The common denominator among all of the good guys with guns is pretty simple. None of them woke up in the morning planning to shoot another person in self-defense. They went about their business prepared to defend themselves and others, but planning to do something is far different than being merely prepared to take action if the need arises.

2: BAD GUYS DON'T GET IT, UNTIL THEY DO

With each successive defensive firearm use in an increasingly armed America, one is almost compelled to sarcastically wonder if bad guys got the memo about the willingness of armed citizens to shoot them.

Maybe they don't read the newspapers or listen to television or radio broadcasts about stories in which a criminal bites the dust or winds up in an emergency room shot by someone he had erroneously picked as a victim. And, according to the most recent update on the number of legally-licensed armed citizens across the country from the Crime Prevention Research Center (CPRC), the odds are going up exponentially that a criminal will face such a confrontation.

The Center, founded by Dr. John Lott, author of such books as *More Guns = Less Crime, The Bias Against Guns* and *The War on Guns*, annually updates this estimate. Their website is loaded with information and data about firearms and self-defense. According to Lott's data, there are more than 17.25 million active carry permits and licenses, and the number is climbing despite predictions that public interest in buying guns and getting carry permits would wane with the election of Donald Trump to the presidency in 2016.

But that's not the way things turned out. Four states reported more than 1 million active carry licenses: Texas, Florida, Pennsylvania and Georgia. Surprisingly, because of the population density, Texas actually didn't make it to the Top 15 when it comes to the percentage of licenses per the adult populations.

Here were the most well-armed states mentioned in the most recent update: The Top 15 states are, in this order, Alabama, Indiana, South Dakota, Pennsylvania, Georgia, Iowa, Utah, Tennessee, West Virginia, Kentucky, Washington, Florida, Arkansas, Colorado and Oklahoma.

And it's not just older white men who have been "arming up" in recent years. According to Lott's CPRC report, more women and minorities are obtaining carry permits. Among women between 2012 and 2018, demand grew 111 percent faster, and among blacks the demand went up 20 percent faster than for whites. Asians also surged ahead in the race to conceal and carry at a rate 29 percent higher than for whites, the report said.

But lest anyone be misled, down in the Lone Star State, the odds are getting lower all the time that a bad guy is going to come in contact with an armed citizen, and the encounter will not end well.

Take the case of Michelle Booker-Hicks, a Texas mom who didn't "demand action" per the gun prohibition lobbying group, she took it when a would-be carjacker jumped into her automobile at a gas station in Dallas when her two sons were in the back seat. The 36-year-old miscreant didn't seem to care about the 2- and 4-year-olds who were waiting while mom dashed inside the station to pay her bill.

But once he was behind the wheel and preparing to make off with her ride and sons, Booker-Hicks didn't waste a second. According to several reports, including one on Fox News – the cable network that doesn't shy away from reporting about such armed-citizen defensive incidents – Booker-Hicks scrambled into the back seat and demanded that the suspect get out of her car and leave.

He made the poor judgment call of not listening, so the mom faced with dire circumstances quickly went to "Plan B." As she explained to a reporter, "I reached over the armrest to get my (gun out of the) glove compartment and that's when I fired at him once."

"I'm not a killer but I do believe in defending what's mine," she said, especially her two toddlers. "I hope that woke him up."

It certainly got the suspect's attention, because she shot the guy in the face. The bullet miraculously didn't kill him, so he was carted off to the hospital for treatment, after which charges were waiting that ran the gamut from kidnapping to carjacking.

Booker-Hicks did not become a wallflower following the incident. Here was a mother with whom nobody in their right mind would care to tangle, and the proof of that was found in an interview she did with KTVT News in Dallas.

"I should have just have emptied the whole clip but I didn't," she said matter-of-factly. "I didn't. I just wanted to give him a warning shot that was it."

Consider him warned!

To keep this story in perspective, Booker-Hicks noted to one reporter that she was not worried about her car, but "about my kids." That's a good thing, because after being shot at point blank range, the carjacker ran her car off the pavement, crashing into a fence.

Of course, such cases have been rare in the past, although self-defense with firearms appears to be on the rise. When the *Washington Post*, which has not been friendly to the Second Amendment or self-defense, looked at self-defense it quoted some researchers who played down such gun uses. One, David Hemenway, director of the Harvard Injury Control Research Center, asserted that a study of five years' worth of data (2007-2011) suggested that the use of guns in self-defense is rare.

Another researcher, Philip Cook, ITT/Sanford Professor of Public Policy and Professor of Economics and Sociology at Duke University, believes the actual number of self-defense gun uses is grossly overestimated. Rather than the estimated 2.5 million defensive gun uses annually that was suggested by research conducted by Gary Kleck and Marc Gertz, criminologists at a Florida university, Cook was quoted in the *Washington Post* article suggesting that the number is far lower.

According to the *Washington Post* article, Cook told the newspaper via email that, "Whenever you're surveying about a rare event like DGUs (defensive gun uses), estimates may well be inflated by the small fraction of respondents who are drunk or deluded or simply having fun."

He reportedly suggested that the percentage of people reporting a defensive gun use in Kleck's survey is similar to the percentage of Americans who say they've "been abducted by aliens."

Whether Cook's remark about "drunk or deluded" people is accurate, or even fair, is a debate for another day. Still, it cannot be denied that defensive gun uses are not so rare as the gun prohibition lobby would have the public believe, and with more than 16.3 million citizens licensed to carry across the U.S., the odds are creeping upward that a criminal is going to encounter one of those armed citizens, and it may not end well.

Illinois experience

When the *Chicago Tribune* dug into the defensive uses of firearms in Illinois, the newspaper discovered something startling. Illinois State Police apparently do not keep track of such incidents.

The newspaper "combed through police files" and found that most people shot by concealed carry license holders were armed robbers, and to a lesser degree carjackers, at least one burglar and a handful of other people. These shootings occurred in all kinds of places, so there is no real pattern insofar as location.

Among things the *Tribune* reported was an observation by State Police Lt. Matthew Boerwinkle: "You rarely hear of an instance where a CCL holder is using their firearm in an unlawful manner. They're generally law-abiding citizens, and they've gone to great lengths to get to where they're at to have a CCL. And they've taken training to get there. And most of them, they understand what the requirements are to use force to defend themselves."

In the years since Illinois adopted concealed carry legislation, there have been several incidents in which citizens legally defended themselves.

In one incident reported by the *Chicago Tribune* after the armed citizen was released by police, the newspaper specifically said the unidentified man as a "concealed carry license holder." The 27-year-old man had been approached by another man one night in December while he was seated in his car outside a variety store.

According to the published account, the armed citizen was approached by a would-be armed robber. There was a struggle during which the citizen fired his legally-carried sidearm, and then he got away from the area, returning a short time later. His bullets struck the alleged robber, identified as a 21-year-old.

Then there was the case of an armed woman who fired in self-defense after being repeatedly stabbed by a 25-year-old man one autumn afternoon, as reported by the *Chicago Sun-Times*. Published reports said the incident occurred in the Lawndale neighborhood.

Identified as Pleasure Cardell Singleton, Jr., the man reportedly stabbed the woman in what was described as a "domestic dispute." Initially, the newspaper said a charge against the woman might be pending, but that didn't apparently get any traction when it became clear this was a case of self-defense.

It's also something of a lesson. Don't use a knife to attack someone who has a gun.

How stupid is that?

It has been suggested that some people enter police work because of the entertainment value of responding to crimes that are by nature the definition of being stupid in public. That's not a felony, nor is it a misdemeanor, but many in law enforcement sarcastically suggest that it ought to be.

Quite possibly the high mark of stupidity was a story in Washington State some years ago in which a would-be robber identified as David Zaback strolled into a popular gun store on Renton's "highland" area and pulled a gun. In order to enter the gun shop, he had to walk directly past a parked King County sheriff's patrol car.

What happened next has been misreported over time, with details often being altered to make the narrative more bizarre, but the facts are strange enough.

It is not clear who fired the first shot, but the sheriff's deputy who was inside, along with an armed store clerk fired the last shots, and they connected.

Zaback announced his intended robbery and told everyone to put their hands on the counter. It was then that he apparently saw the deputy. Zaback fired at least three shots, and both the deputy and the armed clerk fired back, hitting the unlucky robber four times, thrice in the torso and once in the arm.

At the same time, armed customers drew their own legally-concealed sidearms but could not get clear shots, so they did not fire. Four hours after the incident, Zaback died in a hospital, having made what one nationally-recognized firearms authority has dubbed "a fatal error in the victim selection process."

It seems that ever since this incident, bad guys have been testing their luck against good guys with guns, and in a growing number of cases they just haven't fared well at all.

One incident in Tampa, Florida that did not get the attention it deserved involved the attempted robbery of a Sunoco gas station by a man armed with a pellet gun. It was his bad luck that the clerk in that establishment had a very real sidearm, and he used it to shoot the unsuccessful criminal in the leg.

The local ABC affiliate reported that the would-be armed robber "ran across Hillsborough Avenue" to another gas station, with the armed clerk in hot pursuit. It is more likely the wounded wannabe robber hopped, skipped or otherwise limped fast across the street because a bullet wound in the leg is guaranteed to mess with someone's stride.

A reporter captured the common sense remark of Tampa Police Lt. Ricardo Ubinas that put this shooting in its proper perspective: "Now, the clerk knows when you have a gun shoved in your face you don't know if it's a pellet gun or a B.B. gun. It really doesn't change the dynamics of the robber. It's still an armed robbery."

In Hamilton, N.J., two men tried to rob a 7-Eleven one evening, apparently without doing much reconnaissance ahead of time, because there was an armed security guard who, as described by a report in Maxim.com, charged in to ruin their day with a blazing sidearm. A video of the event raced across social media, complete with sound.

The security guard was a rather stout-looking fellow who exhibited absolutely no sympathy at all for the two miscreants he had just shot.

A mother and daughter working at an Oklahoma liquor store put the hurt on an armed robber who, according to various reports, charged into the establishment "brandishing a 12-gauge shotgun" and quickly moved to clean out the cash register.

But what this fellow didn't count on was the game attitude of Tina Ring, 53 and her daughter, Ashley Lee, 30, who were having none of it. When the would-be robber headed for the door, Ring pressed a button that locked the door, and suddenly the predator became the prey. The two women ducked below the counter level for cover, but that's where the fight began. Both women were armed and started shooting, and Ring ended up in a physical battle while Lee tried to get the man in her sights.

Eventually, the bad guy gets up and leaves after the two women had apparently left the shop, and he subsequently drove to a local hospital where he was "put into a medically induced coma," according to a report from *The Sun*.

It came as no big surprise to anyone who followed this story that the suspect, Tyrone Lee (no relation to Ashley) was described as "a serial armed robber" by KFOR News. In an interview with the news station about a month after the robbery attempt, Lee – who was booked into the Tulsa County Jail after his release from the hospital – told a reporter that he "wasn't in his right mind." That much seemed to concur with the thoughts of his intended victims and the police. He was apparently "on drugs and desperate" at the time.

Possibly attempting to compete with Zaback, the slain would-be robber in Renton, Washington, a man identified by published reports in the *New York Post* and a local Fox affiliate in Salt Lake City as Christian Holbert kicked in the door of a house that had a sign on the outside that reads "Smith & Wesson spoken here." The elderly couple living in that home weren't kidding.

Whether the would-be home crasher couldn't or didn't bother to read the sign, as soon as he forced his way in, the man and wife team reportedly shot him. The *Post* story said the wounded suspect completely disrobed and then strolled outside toward sheriff's deputies. They used a taser on him and apparently it had no effect. However, lawmen subdued the man and he was transported by helicopter to the hospital.

Terminal timing

For those who might be planning an armed robbery, timing is imperative to a successful caper, a fact that a would-be stickup man in Indianapolis, Indiana learned the hard way, and he may have lived just long enough to understand that.

In this case, it wasn't just one "good guy with a gun," it was two, and they put a sudden and permanent halt to the attempted armed robbery that unfolded literally right in front of them at a convenience store called the GetGo. The accounts of this crime were reported by the *Indianapolis Star* and WISH-TV news.

Indiana has a long-standing concealed carry law that has more than 860,000 Hoosiers licensed to carry, according to the Indiana State Police. The state also recognizes all other state licenses/permits.

It was a Saturday evening at about 6:25 p.m. when the 26-year-old armed man walked into the gas station and tried to rob the place, having arrived there in what police later determined was a stolen car. Two of the several customers in the store at the time reportedly drew their sidearms and shot the robber, fatally wounding him. He was taken to the nearby Eskanazi Hospital, where the newspaper account said he was pronounced dead.

One local resident quoted by the television report had this sage observation: "Crime doesn't pay, karma is real. You get what you get."

While that lesson may have been lost on the Indianapolis robber, a man who tried to rob the Cozy Corner restaurant in Santa Ana, California will remember because he was felled in one of the strangest citizen intervention incidents in recent times. According to a British news account, the masked robber entered the restaurant, threw a bag at a worker and demanded money.

As the female employee nervously began doing what she was told, a customer who had pulled up to the drive-in window looked inside, saw what was happening and drew his own gun. The armed citizen's bullet connected, sending the robber to the floor. There were at least a couple of rounds fired, and one hit a soda machine, but two more hit the crook.

By the time police arrived, the bad guy had made it across the street, but that was as far as he got. He was taken to the hospital and a woman who was with him at the time was arrested, according to the news account. The armed Samaritan had left the scene.

But the lesson won't help an 18-year-old Cincinnati, Ohio man identified by WLWT News as Anton Kirby, who tried to rob a Hamilton County business but was fatally wounded in the process. This attempted robbery happened at about 10:45 p.m. one night. The robber came into the targeted store wearing a hoodie and blue latex gloves, which is typically a signal that something rather unpleasant is about to happen. Confirmation came with the drawing of a .380-caliber semi-auto pistol.

This time around, however, the clerk at the Harrison Food Mart was legally armed, and after being forced back to the rear of the store to open the safe, the clerk drew his sidearm when the would-be robber turned his head away. Four shots were fired, and they connected. The suspect fled, only to be found outside on the sidewalk by responding police officers.

While it is difficult to fathom why a teen with a clean record might decide to commit a felony crime, that is something for social scientists and psychologists to sort out. The legally-armed citizen – same as a sworn peace officer – does not have the time for analysis of the misbehavior. Their only course of action in those split-second situations is to defend themselves and other innocent bystanders. The criminal made that call, not the intended victim or the armed Samaritan bystander caught by the circumstances.

Then there was Emmanuel Henry, 22, who did have a criminal record. Wanted in connection with nine robberies, according to the *Atlanta Journal and Constitution*, his tenth foray into crime was his last. He made the fatal error of trying to rob someone who had a gun of his own.

Henry's target was a "package store" in Stone Mountain.

According to Channel 2 Action News, Henry ran into the store, leaped over the counter and fired at the clerk while demanding money. Much to his surprise, the clerk pulled his own sidearm and fired back. Henry missed and the clerk didn't.

The would-be recidivist's career ended at a nearby hospital.

Things get embarrassingly difficult to explain in lock-up when you have to tell fellow criminals that you were the unlucky guy who tried to pull a robbery and got shot by a victim, who used your own gun.

That very scenario unfolded at a Durham, N.C. convenience store with a 38-year-old man suffered a gunshot wound to his leg after what WRAL News described as an attempted robbery. The suspect in this case was identified as Kevin White, who apparently strolled into a mini mart with a gun, while using the cover of buying beer to get close to the counter.

Inside the store was a clerk identified as Zaid Omar, who decided he was neither going to be robbed or shot after the suspect pulled his gun and demanded money. Zaid told a reporter that he grabbed the gun from the suspect's hand after struggling with him, and then fired two rounds. It was the first time Omar had fired a gun, but he evidently got the hang of it pretty fast.

Omar said he was in fear for his life, and he grabbed the gun, even though he did not wish to shoot anybody.

And the biggest non-surprise of this story is that the suspect is a convicted felon, so in addition to being shot with the gun he was carrying, which almost certainly was not his to begin with, the charges included possession of a firearm by a convicted felon, WRAL reported.

But in a Milwaukee incident, more conventional events unfolded, according to the local Fox News affiliate. When a 21-year-old would-be robber tried to pull a hold up at a gas station one summer evening, it was his misfortune to pick an armed citizen as the victim. The 33-year-old legally-armed man targeted for robbery drew his gun and shot the thief in the buttocks.

Over the years, countless stories have been told about law-abiding citizens resorting to a firearm to stop a crime.

The common denominator in virtually all of these stories is that Americans fight back, at least when they have the tools to do it, and even sometimes when they don't.

In all of these cases, the criminal element obviously did not count on meeting any resistance, and when it came it was sometimes terminal, and always by surprise. Invariably, that is a reality all of the crooks mentioned in this chapter didn't understand until a few seconds after they stopped a bullet. But by then, it was a little too late to start turning their lives around.

3: THE STUPID IS STRONG AMONG GUN PROHIBITIONISTS

When public officials and/or gun control lobbying groups start talking about "common sense gun reforms," it is almost guaranteed that common sense is nowhere near, and that the "reforms" being suggested are simply gun control with deceptive packaging.

Whether the recommendation is for a ban on modern sporting rifles, all-too-frequently mislabeled as "assault weapons," the proponents quietly hope that most people will believe that such firearms are involved in most of the violent crime in the United States, when the data simply does not support such a conclusion.

A quick check of the annual FBI Uniform Crime Report for any given year will reveal that rifles *of any kind*, including the much-demonized semi-auto models that are so popular among younger shooters, are involved in a fraction of homicides. From one year to the next, rifles are identified as the murder weapon in 2 to 3 percent of all the slayings covered by the FBI Crime Report.

Far more people are killed with knives or blunt instruments or even the bare hands and feet of the killer than are murdered with rifles.

Remember, this is not the Citizens Committee for the Right to Keep and Bear Arms or some other pro gun rights organization talking. It is the FBI and it is difficult, if not downright embarrassing, for the gun control lobby to challenge their data, so they typically do not use it when proposing some new (make that, re-packaged) gun control scheme.

So why are gun prohibitionists so determined to ban the possession of such firearms? It is rather simple, really. The mission is not just to ban a certain class of firearms, it is to get the public used to the notion that banning a whole class of firearms is acceptable. If anti-Second Amendment extremists can convince people that gun bans are okay once, then it becomes less of a chore to promote a ban on yet another class of firearm over the horizon.

With the exception of fanatical anti-gun extremists, Americans are not so gullible as to believe that a ban on firearms will stop criminals from using guns in crime.

The data source that anti-gunners became fond of using over the past 25 years was the Centers for Disease Control and Prevention (CDC), which pushed its way into the gun debate by portraying gun-related violent crime as a "public health" issue rather than a crime problem.

Years ago, Congress passed legislation that prevents the CDC from conducting gun control research, but it didn't prevent the agency from doing a study during the Obama administration that literally blew up in the collective face of the gun control crowd. The result of that particular research is roundly ignored by gun control proponents because it shreds many if not most of their traditional arguments in support of the restriction of the moment.

Perhaps best detailed in an essay that appeared in *Guns and Ammo* magazine, the CDC report – "Priorities for Research to Reduce the Threat of Firearm-Related

Violence" which really looked at a lot of other research – reached the following conclusions:

Armed citizens are less likely to be injured by an attacker. People who fight back with firearms "consistently (have) lower injury rates…compared with victims who used other self-protective strategies." The anti-self-defense crowd never saw that coming.

Defensive gun use is common. The estimates of defensive gun uses range anywhere from 500,000 to more than 3 million annually. In the overwhelming majority of those cases, a shot is never fired. The mere presence of a firearm in the hands of the good guys serves as a great deterrent to violence.

Mass shootings and gun-related accidents are responsible for a fraction of gun-related deaths, according to the report.

Gun controls such as background checks, gun bans and so-called "gun-free zones" produce "mixed results," the magazine noted.

The study also found that "gun buybacks" are ineffective in crime reduction. Still, anti-gunners believe – or at least want the public to believe – that such buybacks (a misnomer, because the government or the anti-gun groups never owned those guns in the first place) do make a difference. And, they make for great sound-bite news stories.

The final conclusion was arguably the most obvious: The majority of firearm-related deaths are suicides, not homicides. Yet the gun prohibition lobby consistently and stubbornly lumps all the fatalities together so they can claim "30,000 deaths annually from gun violence." This is an attempt to create or perpetuate the impression that the country is in the midst of a bloody crime wave.

You Can't Handle the Truth

That famous Jack Nicholson line from "A Few Good Men" perfectly illustrates the dilemma faced by gun control advocates and a largely anti-gun press when facts get in the way of a good narrative. It is especially true when discussing the first finding of the CDC study, that armed citizens who fight back are less likely to sustain an injury compared to crime victims who resort to a different "self-protective strategy."

Nowhere does the argument that a "good guy with a gun is the only thing that stops a bad guy with a gun" cut more directly to the heart of the issue. The "Fight Crime, Shoot Back" philosophy has begun making more sense to Americans who realize that police cannot typically respond in time to prevent or even interrupt a crime, and when it comes to sheriff's deputies in rural areas, they may be at the far end of a 50-mile wide county.

At the time *Guns and Ammo* published its essay, the magazine noted, "The CDC report (was) overall a blow to the Obama Administration's unconstitutional agenda. It largely supports the Second Amendment, and contradicts common anti-gun arguments. Unfortunately, mainstream media failed to get the story they were hoping for, and their silence on the matter is a screaming illustration of their underlying agenda."

The results of the CDC report went largely... unreported by the "mainstream" media, but the report did spread across the blogosphere, where it received lots of exposure.

Although it is getting less rare for a self-defense-with-a-gun story to be kept completely out of the public eye except for localized coverage, when such stories are reported they typically don't last beyond a single news cycle. On the other hand, stories highlighting the criminal misuse of firearms might sustain through multiple news cycles.

Whether this suggests a media bias against the proper defensive use of a firearm by a private citizen depends upon the perspective of the reader or viewer. When *Guns and Ammo* reported on the CDC findings, the magazine noted in conclusion, "The CDC report is overall a blow to the Obama Administration's unconstitutional agenda. It largely supports the Second Amendment, and contradicts common anti-gun arguments. Unfortunately, mainstream media failed to get the story they were hoping for, and their silence on the matter is a screaming illustration of their underlying agenda."

Should this next report get lots of coverage, or just a brief mention? How should the media report this kind of incident?

Seattle's KIRO, the local CBS affiliate, reported that a resident of that city's Ballard neighborhood shot a burglar who was breaking into the man's home early one Sunday morning. According to the published report, the homeowner armed himself with a handgun and proceeded to check his home, discovering that the would-be burglar had broken into the "mudroom" and was trying to enter the main house.

That's when the homeowner fired through the window of the door to the mudroom. After firing, the homeowner called Seattle police. Several minutes later, the report continued, a 35-year-old man with a bullet wound in his mid-section was "dropped off" at Swedish Hospital in the same neighborhood, and was subsequently transported to Harborview Medical

Center, which has one of the best trauma centers on the West Coast.

When police found the getaway car several blocks away, they found blood in the vehicle and standing nearby were a man and woman. Police detained them for questioning, at which time they discovered that the man had an outstanding warrant.

Local government foolishness

Apparently hoping to convince constituents that it was "doing *something* about gun violence," the West Lafayette, Indiana city council passed a "non-binding resolution" – essentially a meaningless gesture – that called for the state "to close loopholes in its gun background check and to ban convicted domestic abusers from owning or buying guns," as reported by the *Lafayette Journal & Courier* after the council vote.

Apparently, nobody on the council understood that there is already a federal law preventing those persons convicted of domestic violence from legally owning firearms or ammunition, and the state also has a law that does likewise. So far as the alleged "loopholes" on gun background checks are concerned, it is never clear what those might be, but it seems to sound good to voters who don't know any better.

Ultimately, this sort of grandstanding doesn't accomplish anything other than creating a false sense of accomplishment when in reality nothing at all has been accomplished. There were reportedly members of the anti-gun Moms Demand Action for Gun Sense in America in the audience that evening, so evidently they went home happy that they had scored some sort of moral victory.

But one member of the council shed a little rain on the parade. The newspaper reported that Councilman Jon Jones abstained on the grounds that the non-binding resolution was "too vague in what policies it seeks."

According to the published report, Jones observed, "The devils are in the details, and I find the resolution lacking in those details."

What the West Lafayette council did understand was that Indiana – like many other states – has a statute that prevents local governments from establishing their own gun control laws. Around the country, many cities and even counties controlled by anti-gun public officials frequently "push the envelope" to challenge, and perhaps even weaken or possibly overturn such laws.

West Lafayette Councilman David Sanders observed during this particular meeting reported by the *Journal & Courier* that, "We have a state legislature who believes in preempting local communities' ability to legislate... This is the fundamental problem." To which fellow Councilman Nick DeBoer added, "I wish we can do more."

West Lafayette is hardly alone in wanting "to do more." In Seattle, Washington, the efforts to either dance around or fundamentally erode the Evergreen State's preemption statute have been ongoing for years. The city has the advantage of free legal help when its efforts are challenged in court, and an activist, billionaire-funded lobbying organization that headquarters in the city and offers citizen initiatives to increasingly restrict the rights of law-abiding citizens in the entire state.

Other municipal governments around the country closely watch the kinds of situations that unfold in West Lafayette and Seattle, primarily to learn from these cases and improve their preemption challenge strategies. It probably isn't part of violent crime reduction plan because in Seattle's case, the data didn't help the argument.

When Seattle hastily adopted a so-called "gun violence tax" on firearms and ammunition in the summer of 2015, the plan was to use the revenues to "study gun violence" and institute programs to reduce it. In 2016, according to Seattle Police Department statistics, there were 18 homicides in the city. In 2017, that number jumped to 27 slayings, not all of which involved firearms, of course.

It is in this arena – the attempts to establish local gun control laws on the argument that they will somehow bring down violent crime rates – that municipal foolishness seems to grow, if not thrive. It bears repeating that criminals do not obey gun control laws, and any expectation to the contrary is the zenith of foolishness. By adopting policies that restrict the rights and abilities of law-abiding citizens to protect themselves and their families, elected officials don't deter crime, they encourage the criminal element, and may even create unintentional criminals in the process.

The political gun control effort in Seattle is a prime example of all of these things congealing. The city in 2017 adopted an ordinance that requires city resident gun owners to lock up their firearms, with fines for a civil infraction if they don't. It's not clear how such a requirement can be enforced short of warrantless searches, but the scheme involves fines against any gun owner whose firearm is accessed without permission and used either to commit a crime or suicide. The fines range from $500 to $10,000.

Anti-gun liberal Mayor Jenny Durkan declared in a prepared statement at the time, "While we can't prevent every gun death or injury, we can take steps to help prevent future tragedies. Requiring that gun owners responsibly store their guns can help make our communities safer places to live."

That city's council unanimously adopted the legislation, which even a columnist for the local newspaper recognized was illegal under the state preemption statute, at least partly due to a study that claimed only 36 percent of Washington State gun owners keep their guns unloaded and locked up. It's not clear how this estimate was developed, since firearm owners are at best reluctant to discuss how or where they store firearms in their homes.

The city was promptly sued by the Second Amendment Foundation and National Rifle Association.

At the same time, a nearby suburban city adopted its own gun control ordinances, and also faced legal action as a result. Perhaps not surprisingly, the state attorney general's office took no action against either community, because Democrat Attorney General Bob Ferguson also supports stronger gun control laws.

When they don't realize they get it

Despite what may seem like an epidemic of foolishness about guns among liberals, especially elected officials, occasionally someone gets things right, typically without realizing it.

In an interview with the *Capital Gazette*, a Maryland newspaper that suffered a mass shooting in the summer of 2018, losing five staffers, U.S. Senator Chris Van Hollen, a perennial gun control proponent, complained that his colleagues on Capitol Hill hadn't done enough to advance the gun control agenda.

Van Hollen advocated legislation such as universal background checks and reducing access to so-called "semiautomatic assault weapons." But like a smart politician, he couched his advice by acknowledging that these and other measures would reduce — but not necessarily eliminate — so-called "gun violence."

Pressed on what other schemes might reduce "gun violence," Van Hollen "pointed to Maryland's permit laws that require homeowners have a permit before purchasing a hand gun," the newspaper reported.

But one need only look at the body count in Baltimore to see how well that has worked. During the previous year, according to CBS News, Baltimore had racked up 343 slayings. Most were shootings, some were stabbings and a few were by blunt force trauma, according to the *Baltimore Sun*.

It was then that Van Hollen offered an explanation that was almost self-contradictory in terms of logic and common sense, but it cut right to the heart of why gun control laws simply have not worked to prevent bad guys from having guns.

"After Maryland passed its permit to purchase law," the senator told the *Capital Gazette*, "you are finding a growing share of out-of-state guns used in crimes. If you are someone who intends to do bad things with a gun, you are a lot less likely to show up at Maryland law enforcement agency and go through a background check."

This is what Second Amendment advocates often refer to as a "Well, DUH" moment. Without realizing it, Sen. Van Hollen had acknowledged that laws and regulations that routinely inconvenience – make that "infringe upon" or "impair" – the rights of law-abiding citizens do not prevent guns falling into the wrong hands. Criminals simply do not comply with the law.

But the senator apparently didn't understand that. He was simply suggesting that because Maryland has some of the most restrictive gun laws in the nation, criminals go around those laws. For example, it is nearly impossible for the average private citizen to obtain a concealed carry permit because these decisions are left to the whim of bureaucrats. But that doesn't stop criminals from carrying without a permit, and Van Hollen was right, they don't go through regular channels to obtain a gun. They get a gun through some illicit means, maybe even in a neighboring state.

There was something else Van Hollen seemed to overlook. When he talked about preventing multi-victim shootings like the one at the *Capital Gazette* offices by "reducing access to semiautomatic assault weapons" he ignored the fact that the newspaper gunman had used a pump-action shotgun.

By no small coincidence, that was the same type of gun that was used by Aaron Alexis, the man who carried out the mass shooting at the Washington Navy Yard in 2013. That shotgun had been legally purchased at a Virginia gun store and Alexis had passed a background check in the process.

The gun prohibition lobby that advocates for a ban on so-called "semiautomatic assault weapons" routinely ignores the fact that rifles and shotguns of any type are used in a fraction of all homicides in any given year, according to the FBI Uniform Crime Report. The count is roughly two to three percent of all homicides, but to hear anti-gunners talk, one would think that rifles and shotguns are demon weapons. This same crime data shows that in any given year, more people are murdered with knives or other sharp implements, and that more people are actually beaten or choked to death than are killed with rifles of any kind.

Perhaps no greater evidence of this came during the confirmation hearings for Judge Brett Kavanaugh to be seated on the U.S. Supreme Court. During questioning by members of the Senate Judiciary Committee, anti-gun California Democratic Sen. Dianne Feinstein argued with Kavanaugh that semi-auto rifles were not in "common use" by private citizens.

There are an estimated 16 million of those rifles in private hands, which Kavanaugh observed would mean they are in common use. Feinstein stubbornly refused to acknowledge this, and she demanded to know how Judge Kavanaugh could oppose a ban on such rifles even after there had allegedly been "hundreds of school shootings using assault weapons that have taken place in recent history?" It was a comment so demonstrably false that even *Reason* magazine took her to task for it in a subsequent report.

As noted by *Reason*, "Feinstein's response was striking for two reasons. First, there have been nothing like 'hundreds of school shootings using assault weapons,' whether you look at 'recent history' or go back half a century. Second, the shootings are irrelevant to the question of whether banning so-called assault weapons is consistent with the Second Amendment."

Feinstein's remarks seemed oblivious to an NPR revelation that a majority of school shootings reported by the U.S. Department of Education "never happened."

"We were able to confirm just 11 reported incidents," NPR reported after a lengthy investigation, "either directly with schools or through media reports. In 161 cases, schools or districts attested that no incident took place or couldn't confirm one. In at least four cases, we found, something did happen, but it didn't meet the government's parameters for a shooting. About a quarter of schools didn't respond to our inquiries."

So, where are these "hundreds of school shootings" involving so-called "assault rifles" of which Sen. Feinstein spoke?

They don't exist anywhere outside the mindset of the gun prohibition movement, evidently. But when the stupid is strong among anti-gunners, facts don't matter and never will.

4: AN INCIDENT IN CICERO

Cicero is a suburb on the west edge of central Chicago, Illinois; the community to which notorious gangster Al Capone moved his operations to escape Chicago police, according to an online history of the city.

With a population of around 84,000, Cicero has had an interesting history, and an incident there in the late summer of 2018 put it on the map once again, because a legally-armed private citizen took the initiative in the middle of a gun battle involving police and an armed parolee from California, saving a wounded cop in the process. That unidentified citizen became a hero, his actions were hailed by the Cicero police chief, and—as one might expect from the editorial page of a newspaper that has not been friendly to the Second Amendment—frowned upon from the perspective that legal concealed carry is not good for Chicago or the state.

What happened in Cicero amounts to something of a textbook case of a good deed turned into sour grapes, not an unusual situation when guns and the proper exercise of force by an armed private citizen is in the spotlight. Anti-gunners, whether in activist groups, as elected officials or seated on an editorial board are loathe to the notion of even acknowledging that armed citizens doing good things is a benefit to the community.

It was a Thursday afternoon just after 5 p.m. when Cicero Police Officer Luis Duarte, 32, was one of two officers trying to pull over a car driven by the suspect, who turned out to have been paroled from California, having been convicted of human trafficking, according to an account by WGN News. The 27-year-old suspect came out of his car shooting a handgun he could not legally possess, halfway across the country from where he should have been. He was wanted on outstanding warrants for parole violation and an alleged sex offense, the news report noted.

The suspect managed to wound Duarte several times before trying to flee on foot, and firing at another pursuing officer.

Into the middle of this mayhem drove the armed citizen, who did not wish to be identified. He had a valid Illinois concealed carry permit and was armed. Having observed the drama unfold right in front of him, that motorist got out of his car with gun in hand and opened fire. At least one published report said the armed Samaritan's bullets hit the suspect, but a different report credited the wounds to bullets fired by one of Duarte's colleagues, who had by then descended on the scene. Even police from neighboring Chicago responded.

Depending upon one's perspective, this is the kind of scenario in which a legally-armed private citizen quite possibly became the life saver, and the key in stopping the fleeing armed felon.

Hours after the shooting, after Duarte had been taken to the Mount Sinai Hospital and into surgery, Cicero Town President Larry Dominick told reporters, "I want to applaud the citizen, a civilian, who risked his life to help in apprehending this armed suspect."

Police commander Jerry Chlada also told reporters, "We were lucky enough to have a good citizen on the street who's a concealed carry holder. And he also engaged in gunfire with the offender who was struck one time."

The local CBS affiliate quoted Richard Schak, identified as a retired Chicago police sergeant and head of the criminal justice program at National Louis University.

"As a general rule," Schak observed at the time, "a person with a concealed carry permit (or any person) can use a weapon to defend themselves from great bodily harm or someone else… In this case I think that citizen is totally justified. And I think he further should be commended because he came to the aid of a police officer who was injured. And in this climate people might be hesitant to do that."

As for the wounded suspect, a Cook County judge observed, "He is the poster child for no bail and that's exactly what he's going to get."

When the 42-year-old armed citizen was interviewed by the local CBS affiliate, he summed things up as being "there in the right time and the right moment. My instincts, you know, told me to do what I did. I didn't think twice to do what I did."

It is rare that a legally-armed citizen gets credit for placing himself or herself in harm's way, especially considering the news media's long history of downplaying this sort of defensive gun use. And that brings us around to the *Chicago Sun-Times* editorial, which was patronizing and somewhat condescending, while criticizing the notion of concealed carry by private citizens.

'If it saves just one life'

There can be no question that the gun prohibition movement practices world-class hypocrisy, especially when one its own popular catch phrases is turned 180 degrees against it. Responding to the shooting in Cicero, which incredibly occurred only days before Chicago hosted the 33rd annual Gun Rights Policy Conference – an event sponsored jointly by the Second Amendment Foundation and Citizens Committee for the Right to Keep and Bear Arms – the *Sun-Times* commented, "A good man with a gun came to the rescue on Thursday of a Cicero police officer. We honor him. But one brave deed does not justify bad public policy."

"Gun control advocates often use some version of the phrase "if it saves one life" in order to justify their ineffective proposals," the NRA responded. The organization continued with this observation:

"Decades of anti-gun messaging has told the American public that if a gun control measure 'saves just one life' any infringement on the rights of law-abiding gun owners is justified.

"For example, in early 2013, President Barack Obama implored Congress to enact gun control by stating, 'If there's even one thing we can do to reduce this violence, if even one life we can save, we have an obligation to try it.' Vice-President Joe Biden reiterated the president's sentiment, noting, 'As the president said, if your actions result in only saving one life, they're worth taking.'

"A pair of older, Chicago-related examples occurred in the 1990s. In 1994, the Cook County Board of Commissioners passed a ban on commonly-owned semi-automatic firearms. Upon passage, Commissioner John P. Daley told the *Sun-Times,* 'If this legislation saves one life, so be it.' In 1998, Mayor Richard M. Daley touted the Windy City's frivolous lawsuit against the gun industry and other gun control measures in an op-ed for the *Sun-Times.* Demanding action, the mercurial mayor wrote, 'One life lost is one too many.'"

It was a measured reaction to an editorial position without much merit beyond a double standard. That's because what happened in Cicero is not an isolated incident; the only such happening upon which concealed carry advocates in the Chicago area can hang their hats.

In 2015, a legally-armed Uber driver had just dropped off his passengers at Chicago's Logan Square when a man later identified as Everardo Custodio opened fire for no explicable reason. The Uber driver drew his licensed handgun and shot Custodio several times. The 47-year-old driver was not charged, and was even hailed for his actions by one local publication.

Nobody else was injured in the incident.

Even the *Sun-Times* acknowledged that a legally-armed citizen had shot a would-be armed robber on Chicago's South Side the previous year, but then it referenced a report by Johns Hopkins University, which receives money from anti-gun billionaire Michael Bloomberg that concluded "that it is a fallacy that 'right to carry' gun laws — whether the gun is concealed or carried openly — save lives and reduce violent crime."

But the newspaper editorial had just refuted that argument by reporting on the Cicero shooting and the other incident!

At the time of the incident, at least 11 people had been fatally shot by legally-armed citizens in Illinois, according to an investigation by the *Chicago Tribune*.

As illustrated in Chapter One, armed citizens all over the map have literally become first responders in numerous shooting incidents in which nobody was injured, or the perpetrator suffered a "life altering" experience that left him seriously wounded or dead. It is both inaccurate and unfair for any newspaper to contend that such incidents, which result in countless saved lives, do not justify what the *Sun-Times* suggested is "bad public policy." It is never bad policy for citizens to defend themselves, their families or another innocent person.

That much became evident in the aftermath of a high-profile self-defense incident at a bus stop in Chicago's Fernwood neighborhood. A 19-year-old would-be armed robber, who had just been out of jail for a couple of months, approached a lone woman who was waiting for a bus. He reportedly drew a gun and demanded money.

Instead, the 25-year-old female pulled her legally-carried defensive sidearm and shot Laavion Goings in the neck, at literally point blank range. Parts of the incident were caught on a nearby security camera that showed Goings running away in one direction and the woman fleeing in another direction to call police.

When Chicago cops showed up, they found Goings about a block away and he was transported to a nearby hospital just in time to be declared dead.

Into this fray jumped the Second Amendment Foundation, reminding the press and the public that had it not been for the landmark 2010 ruling in

McDonald v. City of Chicago, the would-be victim would not have been able to resist.

"A legally-armed 25-year-old woman is alive today because she could fight back," said a SAF news release.

The group noted that incidents such as this one, in which a legally-armed private citizen successfully defends himself or herself, rarely if ever draw a reaction from any of the gun prohibition lobbying organizations, whether Everytown for Gun Safety or its protégé organization, Moms Demand Action for Gun Sense in America. Their silence is such cases is deafening.

Following the *McDonald* victory, SAF initiated a second lawsuit challenging the Illinois ban on concealed carry. It was the final holdout of all the states when its legislature had to literally be dragged kicking and screaming into the 21st Century via the federal court system.

Bloody Chicago

There can be no question that if there is any city in the nation where law-abiding, honest citizens should be legally armed it would be Chicago.

Any municipality that can rack up the kind of body counts common to the Windy City and still find its city administration furiously laboring to keep its citizens disarmed is a city in desperate need of dramatic change, from the top down. Being rid of anti-gun mayors such as Richard Daley and Rahm Emanuel might be a proverbial "good first step," but for the Windy City, much more is needed, including a replacement of the city council.

Chicago has developed a reputation for producing double-digit shooting victims over a holiday weekend, many of them fatalities. In 2017, for example, some 650 people were killed in Chicago, but that number went down the following year to 561 slayings, as reported by local newspapers. Yet, there remains a penchant among the gang element to seemingly regard a year-end homicide total as something of a challenge to be met and exceeded.

Because of the continuing high number of homicides, the Windy City manages to stay well ahead of New York City and Los Angeles when it comes to murders, and the killers don't discriminate on the basis of age or sex. The level of violence might terrify even the likes of Capone or his gangster compatriot Frank Nitti, who at least tried to confine the bloodshed to their own criminal element. The "Roaring 20s" had nothing on the present day, and back then, gangsters even used Thompson sub-machine guns.

For many years, the city banned handguns through clever regulation that did not allow residents to register guns after a certain date. That restriction was nullified in 2010 when the Second Amendment Foundation won a landmark federal lawsuit against Chicago that led to the famous *McDonald v. City of Chicago* ruling by the U.S. Supreme Court.

While the Chicago city government scrambled to make it as difficult as possible for honest city residents to have guns while still barely complying with the spirit of the *McDonald* ruling, the public and Second Amendment groups were determined that the anti-gun regulations would be overcome. That took further court action by SAF.

While all of this legal maneuvering was happening, Chicago continued to log hundreds of slayings.

Consider this for a moment. If one backtracks the annual FBI Uniform Crime Report, it quickly becomes obvious that Chicago sees more homicides in one year than many states report. Much, if not most of the violence is drug- and/or gang-related, with murders committed by people who legally are not allowed to possess firearms, but when has that ever stopped a violent criminal?

It is not surprising that law-abiding citizens want an even playing field. The incident involving the Uber driver and the one involving the Cicero motorist demonstrate that responsible armed citizens can act responsibly when a threat arises.

Ignoring the Facts?

While the media could hardly ignore what happened in Cicero, with the intervention of an armed citizen, there was much less publicity when a group of men identified as "Good Samaritans" by the website Blue Lives Matter, rushed to the aid of a Trenton, Missouri female officer who was shot by a prisoner who was trying to escape custody.

One of those Samaritans was armed, and he held the thug at gunpoint until other police arrived. Accounts of the incident largely omitted the presence of the armed citizen.

Officer Jasmine Diab had been shot in the stomach by the 38-year-old prisoner, identified as Jamey Aaron Griffin. In addition to the charges he was already facing, Griffin was also charged with first-degree assault, armed criminal action and unlawful use of a weapon. He was shot in the hand during the fracas, near the city of Winston.

While the media seemed to ignore the details, a witness identified as Michelle Weller did not. She posted on social media how the "Good Samaritans" saw the physical confrontation between Diab and Griffin, and took the bad guy down.

In a message to Facebook, Weller wrote, "One of these men was armed and was able to defend himself and others without even firing his weapon just by pointing it at the suspect! Because he had his weapon these men were able to grab the suspect, pull him out of the car, and hold him down on the ground until officers arrived on the scene."

Weller subsequently added, "The media doesn't want you to know this because it validates our Second Amendment right to keep and bear arms! They only want you to hear about when guns are used to hurt innocent people so you will believe guns need to be outlawed to save lives but this is a lie, a twisted truth."

One Missouri State Trooper was quoted by WDAF News noting, "I am not advocating that people need to feel that they intervene in a situation this level, however, people chose to and in this situation it was critical."

Why would media reports ignore the involvement of an armed private citizen in the detention of a criminal suspect who had just shot a police officer?

Weller's post also said this: "If it hadn't been for that law abiding citizen carrying his weapon with him for defense, this situation could have ended up very differently and more people could have been hurt. Because he had his weapon these men were able to grab the suspect pull him out of the car and hold him down on the ground until officers arrived on the scene."

Of course Weller's post went viral, racing across social media, shared and re-shared.

Whether her analysis of the media's reluctance to report the armed citizen's involvement was accurate, over the years there has been a tendency to "overlook" such involvement. Today, many people have forgotten or never knew of the involvement of Allen Crum, a private citizen, in the termination of Texas Tower killer Charles Whitman. Likewise, while it is recorded history, there is not often mention of the private citizens who supported law enforcement by helping keep Whitman pinned down with rifle fire while three lawmen and Crum made their way to the top of the tower, where Whitman was killed by officers Houston McCoy and Ramiro "Ray" Martinez.

Samaritans Win Elsewhere

There have been several other occasions, in different states, when armed citizens came to the rescue of law enforcement officers.

In 2017, Arizona State Trooper Ed Andersson was shot and seriously wounded by an apparently crazed individual who had reportedly been firing shots at passing cars on the highway early one January morning in 2017. When Andersson arrived at the scene, he saw a man clutching a woman on the side of the highway, according to CNN, near an overturned vehicle. But the man stood up and fired a round at the trooper, hitting him in the shoulder.

About that time, Thomas Yoxall was driving past. Having been convicted of theft, he had "turned his life around" according to published reports. He spotted the gunman crouched over the wounded trooper, beating him savagely. The original felony charge had been reduced to a misdemeanor, allowing him to retain his gun rights and even carry concealed.

When Yoxall described what happened to a reporter, this is how he explained his actions: "God chose to put me in that place at that particular moment. I just can't see an evil like that perpetuated without intervening."

The armed citizen fatally shot the attacker, later identified as 37-year-old Leonard Penuelas-Escobar. Yoxall was hailed as a hero for saving the trooper's life.

A few months earlier and more than 1,200 miles away, an armed motorist came to the aid of a Florida sheriff's deputy who was being savagely beaten by a man that he'd been pursuing at high speed along Interstate 75. Deputy Dean Bardes was being beaten by a man identified as Edward Strother.

Just then, along came motorist Ashad Russell, who was legally licensed to carry a concealed handgun. He moved in on the melee and ordered Strother to stop punching the lawman. Bardes even asked Russell, who had drawn his sidearm, to shoot Strother. A moment later, the attacker lay on the pavement fatally wounded with gunshot wounds to the neck and shoulder.

Bardes' boss, Lee County Sheriff Mike Scott, praised Russell's actions, calling him a hero.

Both the Arizona shooting and the Florida incident became national news, but not for very long. It was almost as though the press couldn't move on to a different story fast enough, with the exception, perhaps, of Fox News. As mentioned earlier, there seems to be a reluctance by the press to downplay such acts by armed private citizens.

Subsequently, the shootings were considered justified. In Florida, the state attorney's office said Russell was protected by the "Stand Your Ground" law.

What do these stories illustrate to the public? Legally-armed private citizens who go through the process of getting a concealed carry permit or license are not the enemy of law enforcement. Indeed, typically the armed citizen is among the strongest supporter of police and sheriffs, and even though such cases as those in Cicero, Florida and Arizona may be rare, they are not isolated incidents, either.

Back in 2012, in Early, Texas, an armed citizen identified as Vic Stacy grabbed a .357 Magnum Colt Python double-action revolver when he saw a killer, who had just fatally shot two people in the Peach House RV park, open fire on a responding lawman. He watched as murderer Charles Conner fired a rifle at Early Police Sgt. Steven Means.

Published reports say Stacy was about 50 to 60 yards away from Conner, who was firing from behind a large tree trunk, but the armed citizen, 67 years old at the time, was able to get his sights on the gunman and he fired. The bullet struck and Conner fell to the ground where Means was able to shoot him with an AR-15, ending the gun battle. Stacy was later given a rifle by then-Texas Gov. Rick Perry in recognition for his intervention.

An accurate shot of 50 yards with a .357 Magnum revolver is not a difficult feat for some, while others might find it impossible. In Stacy's case, the combination of firearm and the good citizen using it made the significant difference.

In 2015, Ohio resident Dylan DeBoard came to the aid of a Mount Vernon, OH police officer who was being attacked by a homeless man later revealed to be a crystal meth addict. *The Washington Times* noted that Police Cpl. Michael Wheeler was on the receiving end of the attack when DeBoard came up, drew his pistol and held the man at gunpoint as Wheeler was able to put handcuffs on the man.

The following year, DeBoard was honored with the Citizen Award of Valor by Mount Vernon officials.

In another non-fatal incident, a Springville, Utah resident identified as Derek Meyer was driving along when he spotted a confrontation between an unidentified Springville police officer and a man identified later as Paul Douglas Anderson. The officer had been struck in the face by Anderson, and that's when Meyer showed up.

Meyer told Fox News that he drew his pistol and aimed it at the suspect, yelling at him to stop the attack. Anderson immediately ran away, but was later found hiding under a flatbed trailer, the report stated.

A police spokesman told Fox that the armed citizen's actions helped save the unidentified officer's life. As it was, the officer suffered a fractured eye socket and facial lacerations, according to a published report.

In early 2016, another Texas drama was played out in Bastrop, when a legally-armed citizen intervened in an incident in which a local police officer had been disarmed and the thug who grabbed his duty sidearm suddenly found himself staring into the muzzle of someone else's gun.

According to a published report, Bastrop Officer Dylan Dorris had been in a physical fight with a suspect identified as Kenton Sesean Fryer, an Arkansas resident. The incident unfolded outside of a gas station, and the armed citizen, identified as Scott Perkins, saw the fight and drew his sidearm.

When Perkins shouted "Freeze" at Dorris, he became a track star, running from the scene. His freedom did not last long, however, because he was arrested a short time later.

And just to show there are some good women with guns, a case in Dawson County, Georgia found an unidentified woman coming to the aid of Sheriff's Sgt. Randy Harkness, who was being attacked by a homeless man to whom he had given a courtesy ride to a gas station.

When the lawman offered some cash to the homeless man, the physical assault began. The unidentified armed woman, who had been in a car at the gas station, came out of the vehicle and fired. When the homeless man, identified as Justin Foster by Fox News, got up off the sergeant, the woman fired again, and then a third time when the suspect began to flee.

Foster was hit, and he ran to a nearby McDonald's restaurant where he assaulted a 75-year-old woman in the parking lot. At that point, a couple of other customers were able to subdue the wounded man.

Later, Sheriff Jeff Johnson told reporters that he considered the armed woman a hero and that she had probably saved Sgt. Harkness' life.

Beware of the Downside

There can be a downside to being a Samaritan with a gun. The family of the bad guy you shoot can get an attorney and file a wrongful death lawsuit.

Such was the case in Rising Sun, Ind., when Kystie Jaehnen, an armed citizen who witnessed a fight between a state Conservation Officer and a man identified as Justin Holland in February 2017, came to the officer's aid. One year later, Holland's family sued Jaehnen, who had been cleared in Holland's shooting death, along with the Indiana Department of Conservation and officer Michael Powell.

Published reports about the case all concurred about the circumstances. Officer Powell, who was coming off shift, responded to a 911 call about a suspicious vehicle just outside Rising Sun that was partly blocking the roadway and a driveway. That officer soon found himself involved in a struggle with Holland.

Jaehnen saw the fight, grabbed her gun and went to the officer's aid. Powell soon found himself tangling with a man who, according to toxicology reports, had various substances in his system including methamphetamine, dextromethorphan, methadone, marijuana and benzodiazepines. A combination like that might give someone superhuman strength and certainly cloud one's judgment about physically engaging a law enforcement officer, even a game warden. Investigators also discovered meth and other drug paraphernalia, according to a report in PoliceMag. com.

Holland's pickup truck was partly blocking Jaehnen's driveway and the highway in front of her home, one report explained. She fired one round and hit Holland in the torso, fatally wounding him. He was later pronounced dead at a hospital.

Jaehnen and her mother reportedly attempted to provide first aid to Holland, even performing CPR while waiting for an aid crew.

Despite the fact that Holland's family acknowledged that he had been "struggling with demons," according to Blue Lives Matter, they sued. In the aftermath of the shooting, it was also revealed that at the time he was killed, Holland was reportedly facing several unrelated criminal charges.

Jaehnen's supporters started a GoFundMe page to raise thousands of dollars for her defense.

This is the downside of being a Samaritan with a gun, even when law enforcement hails you as a hero and prosecutors decline to file charges.

Aurora Police Sgt. William Halbig, at the time the president of the Laughery Valley Fraternal Order of Police, noted in a fund raising message, "It is tragic how one person's irrational and unlawful actions can destroy the peaceful lives of others."

There's a lot of that going around, which may explain why so many "good guys" are arming themselves. As most self-defense advocates will observe almost by reflex, good citizens don't carry guns in order to kill somebody. They carry guns in order to keep from being killed.

5: A PERSON'S HOME IS HIS/HER CASTLE

Given the public sentiment about defending one's self from home invasion, whether it is a simple burglary or something more dangerous, it's not surprising when public reaction to the shooting of a burglar or home invader by a legally-armed citizen is something akin to a cheer.

Likewise, when someone's business is violently invaded, there is a clear justification to defend one's self and anyone else who is present.

According to a website called "Just Facts," a 1994 study by the Centers for Disease Control and Prevention estimated that Americans use firearms simply to "frighten away intruders who are breaking into their homes about 498,000 times per year. Keep in perspective that this estimate came from a study that was conducted a generation ago, which means that the issue of armed self-defense was just as important then as it is now. It also suggests that while times have changed, the presence of criminals and crazy people in society has remained the same over the timespan of a quarter-century.

An even earlier study cited on the same website polled male felons in 11 state prisons and discovered that 34 percent had, at one time or another, been "scared off, shot at, wounded, or captured by an armed citizen/intended victim. Forty percent had actually decided against committing a crime because they knew or had reason to believe the intended victim was armed.

A whopping 69 percent knew other criminals who had been frightened, shot at or wounded, or captured by an armed citizen/intended victim.

As noted earlier in this book, armed private citizens have accounted for more than 1,000 justifiable shootings of criminals since 2013. In 2017, the most recent year for which data was available at this writing, the FBI Uniform Crime Report says armed private citizens fatally shot 299 people in self-defense. That was out of 353 slayings that were determined to have been justifiable homicides in non-law enforcement cases.

The year before, there were 282 justifiable homicides by armed citizens using firearms, and in 2015, armed citizens fatally shot 272 attackers.

All of those people who were killed had one thing in common, as determined by investigators. They called the play. Whatever else they were doing, it was being done in such a manner as to create genuine fear of grave bodily harm or death in the minds of the would-be victims, or armed Samaritans, who shot them.

Should anyone feel sorry for them? Probably not, since they all had choices, and it is obvious from the fact that their lives were abbreviated that they made at least one really bad choice, and it was their last.

The home is a sanctuary of sorts. It has long been recognized that the home can be defended with all force and ferociousness necessary to "repel boarders," because more than one life may be at stake. Children could be in jeopardy from burglars or other "uninvited guests."

In 2017, according to data from the FBI, there were an estimated 1,401,840 burglaries, which was actually down from the previous year. Burglary accounts for 18.2 percent of property crimes, and of those events, 57.5 percent involved "forcible entry." Residential burglaries accounted for 67.2 percent of all burglaries that year.

Keep in perspective that not all home invasions involve theft of property. In all too many cases, the purpose of such an invasion might be sexual assault, the kidnapping of a child, or murder. Those facts are never lost on investigators or prosecutors whose job it is to sort out all the facts in the aftermath of a residential self-defense shooting. Neither are those facts lost on inquest jurors in the various jurisdictions, who might quietly remind themselves, "There but by the grace of God…"

But none of this apparently matters to the perpetrators of home invasions. Indeed, they may not be thinking about anything specific when they open a window or kick in a door. What they all have in common is that they are, or can be dangerous, and are willing to harm someone in order to commit their crime and get away.

That may have been the case for jail escapee Bruce McLaughlin, Jr., the 30-year-old criminal who was on the lam only briefly in the early hours of a December morning when he made the worst decision of his life to kick in the door of a home near Greenville, S.C. It was McLaughlin's bad luck that on the other side of that door was a slumbering woman who owns a gun, and she knew how to use it.

According to the *Daily Mail* account – that newspaper has an uncanny habit of getting stories about self-defense with firearms in the U.S. sometimes far more accurate than domestic news agencies –

McLaughlin had broken out of the Pickens County Jail with a fellow inmate named Timothy Dill a short time before. They apparently parted company and Dill was picked up quickly by sheriff's deputies.

But McLaughlin evidently had other plans and as soon as he was inside the door of the home he had just invaded, he reportedly grabbed a "knife sharpening tool" and headed toward the female owner's bedroom door.

Somewhere along the way in his criminal career that included about a dozen trips to the county jail on charges that included burglary, grand larceny, drug possession, shoplifting and assaulting a police officer, McLaughlin must have overlooked the fact that in South Carolina, one stands a pretty good chance of encountering an armed homeowner if one crashes through a door at 3 a.m. in the morning.

The woman occupant woke up fast and grabbed her gun. When McLaughlin began moving toward her, she shot him. He was still wearing his bright orange prison garb, which is impossible to mistake for anything but a jail jumpsuit.

According to the newspaper account, Pickens County Sheriff Rick Clark described the dead man as "a big guy." However, a handgun has a way of evening the odds.

"If she hadn't had a weapon there's no telling what would have happened," Sheriff Clark stated. "I gave her a big hug. I told her how proud I was of her."

The British newspaper also quoted the sheriff observing that the armed homeowner provided "a shining example" for why anyone should own a gun and learn how to use it.

"She came out on the good on this end," Sheriff Clark said, "and the bad guy didn't."

That same assessment could apply to an elderly Arkansas woman who put an abrupt end to what may have become a home invasion career involving a 19-year-old intruder who set off an ADT alarm when he made an unwelcome appearance.

According to a local Fox News affiliate, the perpetrator in this case was identified as Cody Smith of Marion. A neighbor of the octogenarian female noted to a reporter that "it makes you be a little more concerned about your neighborhood if have people that are breaking into homes."

It may be slightly less concerning to those neighbors who have guns.

Motor City Mayhem

During the course of a single day in November 2018, the city of Detroit, Mich., reported five homicides. It is small wonder, then, that the "Motor City" – so named for the concentration at one time of all the major automobile manufacturers – has often been considered the most violent big city in the United States.

In 2017, according to the *Detroit News*, the city racked up 267 slayings, which was down from the 303 recorded in 2016. In 2017, the newspaper added, the city logged 13,796 violent crimes, and that was just the number of crimes that were reported. Those crimes included murder, rape, robbery and assault, and that was up slightly from the 13,705 violent crimes reported in 2016, according to the annual FBI Uniform Crime Report.

The Detroit News acknowledged that in 2016, the city's violent crime rate made it the most violent city in the country. In 2017, Detroit dropped to second place on that list; a rather dubious achievement for which nobody held a parade.

But this prelude brings us around to the final moments in the life of a thug who attacked two women who were leaving their home for church services one Sunday morning. It was about 10:30 a.m. when the 55-year-old mother and her daughter were heading out the door when the suspect forced his way inside, according to WXYZ News.

The older woman acted quickly, retrieving a gun and firing two shots at their attacker. One of those rounds hit him square in the chest, and he died on the spot. When police investigated, they determined that the slaying occurred as an act of self-defense, and there were no arrests.

Detroit, while a violent city, has something going for it that other large cities do not. Police Chief James Craig is not what one would call timid on the subject of firearms and self-defense. Back in 2013, Chief Craig caused tremors within the gun control lobby when he famously advocated for concealed carry by Detroit residents. The following year, he gave anti-gunners heartburn when he attributed a stunning 37 percent decline in armed robbery to the fact that more Detroit residents were legally packing.

By one estimate published in the *Washington Times*, there are some 30,000 active concealed pistol licenses in the city. That translates to 30,000 opportunities for an armed thug to make a fatal error in the victim-selection process. Widespread knowledge of this fact just might have a deterrent effect on the city's criminal population, though one might be unable to ever hear a gun control advocate, or even a local politician, publicly consider that possibility.

The newspaper offered what might be considered a typical James Craig quote, "If you're sitting in a restaurant, and you aren't allowed to have a gun, what are you supposed to do if someone comes in there shooting at you? Throw a fork at them?"

And you can bet there were grimaces among anti-rights gun prohibitionists when Craig suggested that legally-armed private citizens in his city treat gun-toting thugs the same as they might a terrorist or a carjacker.

Chief Craig had every reason to suggest that armed citizens are an important part of crime fighting in Detroit. He saw the impact and did not pretend that something else was at play.

Not the Only Place

Detroit is hardly the only place where armed citizens defend their turf, whether it is a home or their place of business, or a location where they just happen to be doing business when criminals come calling.

Take the case of 44-year-old Torrance Battle of Waterbury, Conn. According to several accounts, including one by WTNH, Battle made the fatal mistake of trying to rob an auto sales business in Prospect, Conn. He had a partner who promptly fled when the lead started flying, underscoring the adage that there is no honor among thieves, and evidently courage is in rather short supply as well.

Battle was no stranger to crime, according to various published reports. He had a "lengthy criminal history including several convictions for violent crimes," WTNH said. That would have precluded him from legally owning and carrying a firearm, but gun laws have never been a deterrent to a criminal, especially a recidivist, and everybody knows it.

When Battle and his accomplice entered the business, they reportedly began physically assaulting people inside. That came to an abrupt halt when an unidentified customer drew a handgun, which was legally registered, and opened fire. Battle was hit hard and responding officers found him a short distance from the crime scene, where he was pronounced dead.

A spokesman for the owner of the business told a reporter, "He (the armed citizen) was carrying and he defended himself, and quite frankly saved a lot of lives that night. My clients thought they were going to die and feel extremely grateful for this hero."

Frequently, it should be noted, armed private citizens who use deadly force do not wish to be identified in print. In cases of justifiable self-defense or defense of another person, police agencies routinely keep the identity of the armed citizen confidential and to their credit, most news agencies don't violate that privacy. The armed citizen has done nothing wrong, instead acting within the parameters of the law to stop a violent crime in progress. They have just suffered through a traumatic incident.

Typically, the legally-armed citizen who fires in self-defense is an ordinary person who finds himself or herself suddenly thrust into an extraordinary situation.

For example, there was an incident at a sandwich shop in Ukiah, Calif. According to KRCR News, an armed customer just happened to be in the Subway there one Wednesday evening when an unidentified armed robber tried to hold up the place. Published reports differ a bit, but it appears the armed customer was a firefighter who is licensed to carry, and there was one report that said the would-be robber was armed only with a very real-looking BB gun. The customer probably couldn't tell, but there was some controversy over this one because the armed citizen plugged the bad guy in the butt apparently as he fled the store.

Was this a "clean shoot" as they say in police parlance? The armed citizen reportedly told police he was fearful for his own life and the lives of other citizens.

Police found the wounded suspect on the ground in front of a nearby department store.

In another case in Missoula, Montana, a math professor was alarmed by the sound of sirens in his neighborhood and when he found out the police were looking for somebody, he wisely armed himself with a 9mm Beretta semi-auto pistol and commenced to searching his home for a hiding intruder.

Prof. Josef "Joe" Crepeau, 58, found what he was looking for, according to *The Missoulian* newspaper. Starting in the upstairs, he worked his way down to the basement, where he confronted an intruder in his furnace room. That's when he chambered a round.

Identified as 22-year-old Justin Delaney, the suspect is not the first person to become suddenly docile and cooperative when the action of a firearm is cycled. Crepeau, identified as the chair of the Department of applied Arts and Sciences at the University of Montana and an associate professor of mathematics, turned his captive over to sheriff's deputies.

Underscoring the fact that self-defense with a firearm seems to be an option that is increasingly being used across the country, a man identified as Ralph Byrd Jr., 41, will forever miss his 42nd birthday because he reportedly attempted to burglarize a house in Leavenworth, Kan., and much to his short-lived surprise, the 74-year-old woman who owns the place was home at the time and didn't care to be burglarized.

Still, according to one published report, the incident was so stressful that the woman did suffer a heart attack afterwards. But she survived. Byrd did not.

The *Leavenworth Times* said Byrd was inside the home when the unidentified woman, armed with a handgun, put him down for the count. Responding Leavenworth police officers found Byrd dead on the floor. The homeowner was not prosecuted.

The local prosecutor told a reporter that the law allows a citizen to defend themselves in such cases.

It is almost universally recognized that private citizens who are threatened in their own homes have the right of self-defense and no duty to retreat.

In another fatal encounter of the close kind, a 30-year-old man who stormed into a home in North Bend, Washington ended up in the King County Medical Examiner's office because the 46-year-old occupant of the dwelling had a gun.

Initially identified in some reports as a "burglar," there was quite a bit more to this case than just a desire to steal something. Indeed, it was never established that the dead man had been after any sort of valuables, but he did make some loud threats and literally smashed his way into the home.

With the older man was his girlfriend, who telephoned the sheriff's department for help after the suspect, who was later found to have been under the influence of drugs and/or alcohol, smashed through a sliding glass door and charged inside, yelling that he would kill the occupants. The couple had locked themselves in the bedroom, and the man advised the intruder that he was armed.

That didn't deter the younger man, who started pounding on the bedroom door, finally knocking it down. That's when the older man fired.

The dead man was later identified as Joshua Shane Henderson, and it was apparently not the first time he had behaved in such a manner. He had previously pulled a six-month jail sentence in Eastern Washington's Benton County, about 200 miles away, after having broken into a home while intoxicated. This time, however, he misbehaved with the wrong people.

When a 32-year-old man apparently broke into a home in California's Lucerne Valley just after midnight, the female homeowner was awakened by her barking dog. The woman entered a bedroom to find the suspect hiding there, yelled at him and then retreated to the living room, where she "armed herself with a gun," according to an account on a local Fox News affiliate in Los Angeles.

When sheriff's deputies arrived, they found the suspect with a gunshot wound that proved to be fatal. The homeowner told investigating lawmen that the intruder approached her even after she yelled at him, and "fearing for her safety," she fired one round. It struck home.

What this case demonstrates is that even in California, with some of the more offensive gun control laws in the nation, a homeowner—especially a female—is still able to fire in self-defense when in genuine fear of imminent and unavoidable threat of grave bodily harm or death.

The report noted that investigating detectives found evidence that the man had forced his way into the home.

Investigators with the Marion County, Fla., Sheriff's Department had all sorts of evidence of a home invasion when they arrived at the scene of a violent confrontation in the community of Summerfield. They found 21-year-old Keith Jackson Jr., dead, 22-year-old Nigel Doyle fatally wounded, and the homeowner also wounded. However, that 61-year-old homeowner was armed with an AR-15 rifle, which leveled the playing field, as it were. According to published reports, two other suspects were arrested near the scene.

Doyle, who died later at a hospital, was found with a shotgun lying next to him on the ground. Near Jackson was a handgun, according to a report in the *Herald Tribune* newspaper.

The homeowner, who was reportedly disabled, had been aroused from sleep by a crash. His rifle was next to the bed and he opened fire as two of the suspects rushed toward him.

Worthless Protection Orders

Following the 2015 brutal slaying of Carol Bowne in New Jersey's Berlin Township by an ex-boyfriend against whom she had not only taken out a protection order, but also applied for a permit to buy a handgun for home protection, there was considerable public debate among conservatives about the effectiveness of such orders.

Bowne's murder wasn't the only case in which a protection order proved to be nothing but a worthless piece of paper. The fact that the Berlin Township police department literally allowed her permit application to gather dust for weeks raised some fury among a couple of evening commentators on Fox News, but did not go far beyond that.

The 39-year-old Bowne was repeatedly stabbed in her driveway and left there to die by the boyfriend. He was later found hanged in a nearby garage, an apparent suicide.

About four years later in Cincinnati, Ohio there was another case involving a woman who had taken out a protection order against an ex-boyfriend. But in this instance, when he tried to kick his way into her home, causing her to fear for her own life and the lives of her five children, this woman grabbed her legally-owned handgun and shot the attacking ex.

To his credit, Hamilton County Prosecutor Joe Deters quickly determined that the woman acted within the law and in fear for her life. And he probably caused no small degree of angst among gun control proponents when he declared in a statement, "Thank goodness she had a Concealed Carry Permit and was able to defend herself and her five children. It is hard to imagine what might have happened to her or her children if she had not been able to protect herself and her family."

This seems like the proverbial "no-brainer." Yet, there are anti-gunners in this country who would decry what that mother did, contending that she should have called police and waited. These glass bubble safety experts evidently have little experience with real-world situations in which one does not have the time, or the opportunity, to dial 9-1-1 and wait.

In an online blog, a man named Gary Direnfeld summed up the false sense of security provided by a protection order.

"People are cautioned not to believe that a protection order actually provides protection," Direnfeld observed. "It does not. It can in some instances improve the likelihood of one's safety, assuming the person subject to the Order actually follows the Order."

Burglary in Progress

Police and sheriff's deputies almost universally respond quickly to reports of burglaries of occupied residences due to the potential that lives may be at stake. Depending upon the jurisdiction, a response could take minutes or maybe longer, because some areas might have lawmen and women working at some distance from where the offense occurs.

That may or may not have occurred to a Kentucky homeowner who had the misfortune of encountering—all too briefly as it turned out—a man identified by authorities as 43-year-old Joshua Kersey of Cincinnati, Ohio. The homeowner, identified as Floyd Gillie, Sr., was at home with his wife. Unfortunately for the bad guys, Gillie's 24-year-old son was also there.

According to a published report in the *River City News*, Kersey and two "accomplices" entered Gillie's home, armed and apparently not in good moods. They wore ski masks and they were looking for someone who had not lived in the home for several years, the newspaper said.

Gillie and his wife were threatened, and that's when Floyd Gillie Jr. grabbed a handgun from an upstairs bedroom. As Kersey and the other two advanced toward the bedroom, the younger Gillie fired. Kersey was fatally wounded but he made it all the way outside before collapsing as his companions made a hasty departure.

Kentucky has a "Castle Doctrine" law that covers this sort of event. The story quoted Kenton County Commonwealth's Attorney Rob Sanders, who explained matter-of-factly, "Mr. Gillie was justifiably in fear for his safety and the safety of his parents. So he was entitled to use deadly force in defense of their home."

A fitting summation in this case was supplied by Republican Congressman Thomas Massie, who suggested in a tweet message that people like Kersey "should think twice."

In this case, he may not have even thought once, and that was all the chances he had.

"Castle Doctrine" laws essentially cement the principle that a person's home is their "castle," to be defended against burglars and other home invaders. They establish that there is no duty to retreat from such a home invasion. The late Mr. Kersey is not the only person to run afoul of such a law.

When a neighbor of Missouri resident Benjamin Seadorf let out what was described by Fox News as a "blood curdling scream," he prudently grabbed his 9mm pistol and ran to her assistance. What he encountered next was a scene which obviously stunned him. The neighbor woman was screaming for help, her clothing was in tatters and at least partly ripped off, and there was a man standing over her.

Seadorf leveled his handgun's sights and ordered the suspect out of a car in which the violent attack had occurred. Then it was down on the ground until Kansas City Police arrived, which was a short time later. The suspect was carted off to jail.

Not all cases of Samaritans acting to help women turn out so well. There was a nationally-reported case involving a fatal stabbing at the Seattle Center, after which the man responsible found himself staring into the muzzle of a legally-carried handgun.

The armed citizen was identified as Scott Brown, who was working at a food stand in the Armory building. A man later identified as David Lee Morris fatally stabbed Gabrielle Garcia, 28, as the couple's 5-year-old son watched. She had filed for a protection order against Morris, but as the saying goes, a fat lot of good that did.

Brown quickly pursued Morris, who walked outside, and confronted him with gun drawn. The incident was captured on video, and it went viral. The courageous armed citizen kept eye contact with the suspect and eventually another citizen, armed with pepper spray, gave Morris a good dose of the irritant that kept him distracted until police arrived.

In the case of a Sebewa Township, Mich., shooting, the police didn't arrive until after it was too late. A man identified by the *Lansing State Journal* as Justin Eddy was killed in a confrontation with an unidentified homeowner in Ionia County, more than 100 miles northwest from Detroit. According to published reports, when Eddy forced his way into the home, he told the homeowner that he was being pursued by someone who was allegedly trying to kill him.

The homeowner armed himself and went outside with Eddy, the newspaper reported, but saw nobody. Back inside, the report continued, Eddy became erratic and angry, assaulting the homeowner who then fired.

Adding to the complicated story was the fact that Eddy drove to the home in what turned out to be a stolen vehicle, taken from a home about two miles away. Authorities found Eddy's pickup truck there, apparently with the motor running.

Canceling car theft

Depending upon which part of the country in which one resides, it may or may not be legal to use deadly force to prevent a thief from escaping with your car, since the issue is property crime and not generally considered a life-threatening offense.

The owner of a car could be subjected to criminal prosecution for taking the life of a car thief who was driving away and not posing an immediate danger.

Surprisingly, a number of incidents in which a car owner wounds or kills a thief have occurred in Washington State, and one case several years ago that resulted in a jury trial ended in acquittal for the armed homeowner who fatally shot a man named Brendon Kaluza-Graham. There was something of a bizarre side effect of that shooting, according to a report broadcast at the time over KHQ.

Quoting Spokane Police crime data, in the seven days following Kaluza-Graham's death, auto theft reports jumped 15 percent in the city. Yes, one would think just the opposite effect would have been reported, but that's not the way it was.

This case caused some interesting tremors in the Evergreen State legal system, and perhaps reflected a hardline shift in public opinion.

Kaluza-Graham was reportedly driving away in a car belonging to Gail Gerlach, who had been warming up his SUV one cold March morning. While law enforcement agencies and insurance companies both caution people against this practice, and in some jurisdictions an officer can issue a citation for doing it, in parts of the country where the mercury can dip into the single digits or low double digits even as Spring approaches, people still like to warm up their vehicles.

The other side of this dilemma, of course, is that a person's property should be left alone. If it does not belong to you, keep your hands off of it and stay out of it.

Gerlach was charged with manslaughter for having fired the shot that killed Kaluza-Graham as he motored down the street in Gerlach's vehicle. As noted by the *Spokane Spokesman-Review*, the jury determined that Gerlach neither acted recklessly nor negligently when he fired. The dead man's family was upset that Kaluza-Graham never had a chance to present his defense.

At the far end of the state a few years later, a homeowner in Aberdeen, a city on the Pacific Coast, shot a 28-year-old suspected car thief in the leg for allegedly trying to steal a car on Christmas morning. According to KBKW, the 54-year-old homeowner found the suspect allegedly attempting the theft and confronted him. When the younger man reportedly lunged at the car's owner, he fired and the bullet wounded the would-be thief in the leg.

Another suspected car thief was not so lucky, however. As reported by KOMO, the Seattle-affiliate of ABC News. A man identified as Blake Moore, 27, was fatally shot while breaking into a pickup truck belonging to a Maple Valley resident, a community several miles southeast of Seattle. Making matters worse, the suspect and his girlfriend reportedly drove to the crime scene in a stolen Honda that was fitted with stolen license plates.

Of course, Washington does not have exclusive domain over auto theft or incidents that result in a would-be thief taking a bullet rather than a vehicle. But as happened in Spokane, these unfortunate adventures can include being arrested, even if there is no prosecution.

A Memphis, Tenn., woman was briefly taken into custody after she shot a man who was breaking into her car one chilly December morning. But she wasn't in custody long and the only criminal charges were leveled against the man she shot, identified by WREG as Jhatavieus Corley. He allegedly had attempted to break into other cars parked around the Brentwood Place Apartments but whatever he was doing came to an abrupt halt when a female car owner put a bullet into him.

The woman subsequently told investigators that she was in fear for her life.

A story about the incident quoted Chip Holland, director of training for Range USA. He told a reporter that under Tennessee law, one does not have the right to shoot unless there is fear of grave bodily harm or death. Shooting someone for merely stealing property is not allowed, so there must be a genuine degree of fear for personal safety before a trigger can be pulled.

This principle was first explored in depth more than 30 years ago in a book that has become something of a classic, *In the Gravest Extreme*, by Massad F. Ayoob. You cannot use lethal force in response to a less-than-lethal threat, but you can use such force in a life-threatening attack. It will be up to investigators and prosecutors to determine whether a deadly force shooting is justifiable.

Seniors survive

"Good guys" with guns come in all sizes, shapes and...ages. And there is one lesson that criminals never seem to grasp: Old people often didn't reach their golden years by simply being lucky. They make it that far not by being stupid or easy, but by being able to take care of themselves, and whatever trouble that comes along.

According to the FBI Uniform Crime Report for 2017, West Virginia that year reported 79 slayings including 45 that involved firearms. It's not an alarming rate, and indeed it might reflect the fact that West Virginians aren't in the habit of allowing people to break into their homes for whatever reason.

Just ask the authorities in Hillsboro, who responded to an early morning call to the Seneca Trail neighborhood, where they found a 34-year-old Marlinton man lying in the front yard of a home he allegedly had tried to break into before he found out that the 70-year-old female homeowner had a .22 Magnum rimfire rifle and knew how to use it.

The .22 Magnum is a potent little cartridge, and has been used by hunters over the years to take predators all the way up to bobcats and even mountain lions on a few occasions. The bullets are small and weigh only 30 to 50 grains, but when they launch out of a gun muzzle at up to 1,500 feet-per-second, whatever is on the receiving end is going to hurt.

In the West Virginia case, the would-be home invader found out the hard way that being shot by an elderly woman hurts more than one's pride. And a trip to the hospital for treatment is normally followed by another trip to the nearest jail.

Perhaps not surprisingly, neighboring Pennsylvania has a lot more crime, including murder, than West Virginia, which is explained by the presence of Philadelphia and Pittsburgh, and a few other large cities, and a considerably larger population. In 2017, the Keystone State reported 735 homicides, of which 567 involved firearms, according to the FBI annual crime report.

An incident in Wayne County, in the state's northeast corner bordering New York, saw a 36-year-old break into the home of a 90-year-old man named William Gabriellini. For his troubles, the burglar collected a gunshot wound in the leg and an arrest.

According to a report broadcast by the local Fox News affiliate, the suspect in this little drama may have seriously underestimated his intended victim.

The report quoted Pennsylvania State Trooper Robert Urban, who observed, "Basically what happened is it's kind of an example of how the Castle Doctrine works. A law-abiding citizen has the right to protect themselves inside their home or their vehicle if their life is threatened, and that's exactly what Mr. Gabriellini did."

The younger suspect evidently didn't consider the possibility that the older gent might have a gun handy. He probably didn't realize that many people in their 90s are light sleepers, so breaking into a home at 3 a.m. on a Friday morning is no guarantee of success.

A report on the incident also quoted the operator of an indoor shooting range in Honesdale, the community where Gabriellini lives. Graceann Anderson told a reporter that the older man "refused to be a victim. He is able to survive and have a day again tomorrow. That's what a firearm does. It protects anyone who refuses to be that victim."

After police arrived, they carted off the wounded suspect to a nearby hospital for treatment.

A range safety officer identified as Zachary Travis offered this observation: "When at that age, it's a good thing to be able to rely on a firearm, because they are not as strong or have the ability to defend themselves. It gives them an upper hand, so it's a good thing to think about for elderly people."

Tangling with people in Pennsylvania or West Virginia may have its risks, but when four would-be outlaws broke into a home in Yuma County, Arizona, they discovered quickly just how risky it can get in a state where a large segment of the population is armed.

According to KYMA and a report in the *World Tribune*, an unidentified homeowner was asleep early one January morning when the four intruders made the mistake of trying to break in. The subsequent shootout left three of the home-breakers wounded, and one, identified as Jessica Aynes, was killed.

What was stunning about this case, according to the published report, is that the intended victim even tried to alert his unwelcome visitors that he was home and awake by flipping his house lights on and off to scare them away. But incredible as it may seem, the break-in proceeded and the shooting erupted.

Arizona is a "stand your ground" state, which means that citizens are not required to retreat from a threat, especially in their own homes. And being in the Southwest, where the western tradition of self-defense remains strong and well more than 300,000 people are licensed to carry in a state that doesn't require a license to carry, the odds of being shot by an intended victim in Arizona increase exponentially.

It is much the same in Alabama, where the biggest difference may be in the accent. Everything else is pretty equal, especially the desire to be left alone by unsavory types.

Just ask 75-year-old Marcia Black, whose interesting experience was reported by Fox News.

When a man on the run identified as Cameron Powers crashed a stolen car near her Limestone County home west of Huntsville, Ms. Black grabbed a smallbore scoped rifle and went out to confront the fellow. She asked if she could help the man, but when he said he wanted to use her telephone and advanced in her direction, the septuagenarian fired a shot in the air to discourage him.

"He knew I meant business," Black said in an interview.

Even the muzzle blast of a .22-caliber semiautomatic rifle can be startling, and it was Powers' good luck that he dropped to his knees until local lawmen arrived to put him in handcuffs, at which point he attempted to run, but didn't get very far.

What Black's case represents is more typical of the defensive uses of a firearm than the shootings we've discussed here and in other chapters. Powers got a ride to jail. He could have just as easily gotten a ride to a hospital or the morgue.

6: NONE DARE CALL
THEM 'VIGILANTES'

According to one online definition, the term "vigilante" applies to "a member of a self-appointed group of citizens who undertake law enforcement in their community without legal authority, typically because the legal agencies are thought to be inadequate.

Many years ago, the film "Death Wish" starring the late Charles Bronson told the tale of a New York architect who, having lost his wife and seen his daughter catastrophically injured in a home invasion robbery and sexual assault, became something of an avenging angel. Armed with a .32-caliber revolver given to him by a client, Bronson covertly began roaming the streets, killing thugs that preyed on honest, but defenseless, citizens.

The plot had police and New York press dubbing Bronson's Paul Kersey character as "the vigilante." According to the story, crime began dropping as a result of the Bronson character's overnight activities, but police didn't dare admit it out of fear that there would be copycat killings and because city government simply didn't want to admit that "the vigilante's" activities were having a positive effect.

The film was updated years later, with Bruce Willis taking on the Kersey role, switching occupations from architect to doctor. Still, his "vigilante," like Bronson's original character, was ultimately allowed to go free by police. That part of the plot line didn't change much.

With a "vigilante" on the streets, the criminal element was behaving itself better.

But in recent years, the term "vigilante" has been used to malign people who have been forced by circumstances beyond their control to defend themselves or other persons who face grave bodily harm or death at the hands of criminals. In other words, the term, itself, takes on a derogatory tone as though the person labeled a "vigilante" has appointed himself or herself as the proverbial "judge, jury and executioner" as depicted by Bronson and Willis in their films.

In a growing number of cases, however, legally armed private citizens who have come to the aid of their neighbors, friends, family or total strangers are frequently appreciated for their courage and selflessness. They are occasionally called "heroes" by a sheriff or police chief, especially if they have intervened in a situation in which a law enforcement officer was in jeopardy.

We talked about such citizens in Chapter 4, and there are countless numbers of private citizens who have literally "put it all on the line" when seconds counted and the police were minutes, or longer, away.

According to a report in AmmoLand, there could be as many as 500,000 to 3 million defensive gun uses ("DGUs") annually. The actual number is "difficult to measure," the popular online firearms news site said. It is probably impossible, while the article alluded to the National Self Defense Survey that estimated approximately 2.5 million DGUs in 1993. That was more than two decades ago, and there is little doubt that with expanded gun ownership and a considerable rise in the number of carry licenses across the state, the annual data has risen with the tide, so to speak.

If one considers that the law ultimately rests in the hands of the people, then it at least appears justifiable for the armed citizen to intervene in what can only be defined as a "life or death" situation.

In 2013, the FBI released a report on "active shooter" incidents, looking at 160 such cases that occurred between 2000 and 2013. Of those, five involved legally-armed citizen intervention in which three shooters were killed, one was wounded and one took his own life. That fact was alluded to by WJHL News in Tennessee when it reported about a case in Sullivan County in which an armed citizen emerged as "a hero," according to the report.

The story quoted Sheriff Jeff Cassidy, who said that the gunman entered a dentist's office and shot his (the gunman's) wife. But the unplanned outcome unfolded quickly when an armed "bystander" drew his own gun and shot the suspect. That armed citizen then held the shooter until police arrived.

It's not "vigilante justice" for an armed citizen to return fire when he or she suddenly are in the middle of an extraordinary event. As noted in Chapter One, the incident in Oklahoma City that involved a man opening fire at a popular restaurant erupted in an immediate response from two armed citizens who apparently did not know one another, but could recognize a public safety threat and responded accordingly.

Some might argue that mass shootings are becoming more frequent because so many Americans have guns, but the flip side of that is to acknowledge that armed citizens have at least been able to respond to some of those incidents and stop them.

As if to underscore that potential, a report from Kansas involving a shootout between an armed citizen and a group of armed robbers included a quote from Wichita Police Lt. Chris Halloran in which the lawman observed, "In our state here in Kansas, we do have open carry and carry concealed. So individuals breaking the law may never know when someone in line at a store, in this example, (has a gun). That's what happened in this case."

The case to which Lt. Halloran was referring occurred one Friday afternoon in December when the would-be robbers entered a convenience store in South Wichita. The crooks demanded money from the cashier and also robbed the armed citizen, who then drew his gun and opened fire. Three of those suspects fled but the fourth took a bullet to the head and was still at the crime scene when police arrived moments later. That suspect was taken to a local hospital.

Some people might argue that the armed robbers posed no threat, which would be nonsense. Whenever a criminal is aiming a gun or waving one around, that constitutes a lethal threat whether anyone actually says anything or remains silent. The visible threat is unmistakable: Cooperate or risk getting shot, perhaps fatally.

Although self-defense experts and instructors will uniformly caution people not to draw "against a drawn gun," when a person is faced with what conclusively is an immediate and unavoidable threat there are really only three choices: flee if possible, fight for your life or curl up and possibly die while begging for mercy, which is a quality not typically found among violent thugs.

And what is a "violent thug?" That's someone who aims a gun at you or threatens with a knife or some other potentially deadly weapon and demands money or something else you have that he wants.

Potential battlefields

The aforementioned FBI study of the 160 active shooter incidents included 73 (45.6%) cases that unfolded in "areas of commerce." Translation: Private businesses. These include businesses open to pedestrian traffic and those that are closed to such traffic, such as offices and other closed businesses.

Another 39 happened in education facilities, frequently called "soft targets" because they are considered to be "gun-free zones," except for the fact that violent shooters have yet to respect the firearm prohibition. Indeed, preventing law-abiding citizens from carrying guns legally in any place often translates to creating a risk-free and target-rich environment where there would be no risk of armed resistance.

As already detailed in earlier chapters, there are several examples of legally-armed private citizens confronting dangerous criminals.

For example, an armed robbery in Turkey Hill, Pennsylvania went bad for the perpetrator when a legally-armed citizen intervened, according to a local Fox News affiliate. The suspect was identified as Lawrence Galloway, and at the time of this caper, he was reportedly wanted for a parole violation and there was an "active criminal warrant" in Harrisburg for his arrest, which had to do with a drug possession charge.

The robbery added to his troubles. The armed citizen saw the robbery in progress and entered the store, confronting Galloway and subsequently shooting him several times. The wounded suspect was hauled away to the hospital.

At the time of this writing, Pennsylvania was one of four states with more than 1 million active carry licenses, according to the Crime Prevention Research Center. The other three are Florida, Georgia and Texas.

Most crime involves more personal incidents rather than mass shootings, which remain rare in the United States despite media sensationalism to the contrary. Quite often, no shots are even fired by the intervening "good guy with a gun."

When a security guard approached two suspected shoplifters at a Loomis, California grocery parking lot, one of them pulled a knife and attempted to stab the guard, according to a report published by MSN. But a legally-armed "good Samaritan" intervened, drawing a gun and ordering the woman holding it to drop it.

The female and her male companion were taken into custody by responding Placer County Sheriff's deputies.

According to the report, it was the male half of the duo who initially pulled the knife, which fell out of his hand during a physical altercation with the guard. The male suspect told his companion to grab the knife and stab the guard, but as she was moving toward her intended victim, the armed citizen appeared and stopped her cold.

What this incident demonstrates is that an emergency situation can happen literally anywhere. The question is whether you want to depend on some armed citizen coming to your aid, or be an armed citizen capable of being your own first responder.

Don't expect to be universally acclaimed for acting to stop a violent situation. In the aftermath of the Loomis incident, a spokesperson for the grocery chain expressed gratitude for the action of the security guard "and for the good Samaritan who offered additional support."

Down in Miami-Dade, an incident involving an armed robbery and a food truck driver who happened to have a sidearm brought this reaction from a police detective: "We are very fortunate that this incident was not any more tragic than what it turned out to be. This is not something that we condone and we don't ask anybody in the community to do this. Please do not confront any individual that is armed."

Sometimes, avoiding a confrontation simply is not an option.

According to the local NBC affiliate, the food truck driver found himself face-to-face with the armed robber. The suspect in this caper reportedly approached the food truck and aimed a gun at Oria Chirino who was inside the truck. Identified by another report as Miguel Diaz Lozada, 58, the driver "heard the commotion and came around" the truck to find out what was happening. At that point, the robber aimed a gun at Lozada, who was handing over some money when he pulled a gun and fired.

When a second suspect attempted to flee, a bystander tackled him and held him on the ground until police arrived.

But that wasn't the end of things. The armed robber ran to a nearby parked car and fired shots at the truck driver and he returned fire, wounding the gunman. He subsequently showed up at a local hospital and police rounded up the third suspect.

When the media reports such incidents, they frequently refer to the armed citizen as a "gun-wielding good Samaritan." Perhaps that is more politically correct than simply identifying the good guy with a gun as a "legally-armed private citizen."

One such individual was lauded but unidentified when an armed Massachusetts resident put a halt to a road rage incident that involved a scene that could have come straight out of Hollywood. According to Fox News, a 37-year-old man was held at gunpoint after he was stopped from driving down a highway with a 65-year-old man identified as Richard Kamrowski clinging to the hood of the speeding SUV.

This bizarre incident began when the SUV driver and Kamrowski had been exchanging insurance information following a minor accident on Interstate 90, the freeway that stretches all the way from Boston to Seattle, Washington. When the SUV driver started to drive away, Kamrowski reportedly jumped on the hood as the vehicle sped up and then slowed down, apparently trying to get the 65-year-old to slide off.

But Kamrowski hung on for about three miles with speeds climbing to an estimated 70 m.p.h., according to the published report. Finally, the mysterious armed stranger intervened, and the incident came to an end. But not everything went well because Kamrowski was subsequently charged with disorderly conduct, while the man who tried to flee was reportedly charged with assault and several other counts.

There was an incident in Chicago worthy of mention here. While the Windy City is infamous for the body count from criminal homicides, sometimes the good guys with guns win the day. That was the case when a 67-year-old legally-armed private citizen was approached by a much younger man one afternoon while he was unloading his car behind a business. According to WLS News, the local ABC affiliate, the young man struck his intended victim on the head and in the face in an effort to steal his property.

What the thug obviously hadn't included in his plan was getting shot, but that's exactly what happened when his victim drew a handgun and fired. The robbery suspect was hit and was transported to the hospital, according to the report.

Bad Business

Most business establishments have strict policies that forbid employees from carrying guns on the premises. Such policies have occasionally resulted in the death of an employee, so not everybody follows the rules.

The business is looking at reducing liability. The employee simply wants to go home alive at the end of his or her shift. In the aftermath of a shootout, if an armed employee is still alive, they are often fired for violating company policy. Presumably that's the punishment for not allowing one's self to be murdered on the job.

But there are some happy endings. When a pair of individuals tried to rob a Las Vegas jewelry store late one Saturday afternoon, they took the trouble to try tying up a customer and several employees. However, they missed somebody. According to the local Fox News affiliate, an employee in the rear of the shop had a gun and he came out and opened fire, killing one of the suspects while sustaining more than one bullet wound. One of the customers was also hit in the exchange.

The other suspect fled the scene.

In such a situation, it may never be known what might have occurred had not the armed employee intervened. The thieves may have left with their stolen goods and not harmed anyone. On the other hand, they might just have decided to not leave witnesses.

Sometimes, armed intervention is provided by a customer in some business. That happens occasionally, and it's usually the robber who gets the worst of it.

When an armed robber tried to hold up a McDonald's fast food establishment in Houston, Texas, he probably never expected that he would encounter an armed customer. As reported by KPRC News, this caper unfolded one Friday evening in the northwest part of the Gulf Coast city.

The would-be robber aimed a gun at an employee and that's when the armed customer drew a handgun and shot the bad guy. Wounded, the robber fled on foot but showed up later at a hospital, where he was promptly arrested by police.

It didn't turn out quite as well for a Philadelphia thug who tried to rob a store on the city's west side. According to KYW Newsradio, the 20-something suspect entered the store wearing a ski mask and carrying a gun. That's usually a visual signal that something bad is about to occur, and the store owner reacted quickly, drawing his own sidearm and shooting the would-be robber in the stomach area.

Although the suspect managed to stagger out of the store, he was found a short distance away and transported to a local hospital, but succumbed to his wound.

A private security guard wound up being the "good Samaritan" one night at a Huntsville, Alabama nightclub, and she was called a hero by police after what was a harrowing experience. Identified in one report by WAAY News as "Latoya," the female security officer found herself up against a felon in possession of an AK-47 after he had been booted from the nightclub following a fight.

The suspect, identified as Samuel Williams, went to his car and retrieved the rifle, subsequently opening fire. As Williams reportedly moved toward the door of the club, where he might have easily wounded or killed several people, the female guard took cover and opened fire, hitting the suspect at least once.

What followed can only be called a "class act" on the part of the security officer. She went inside the club to retrieve a trauma kit she kept inside the club, in order to render first aid to the man she had just shot. However, by the time she came back outside, Williams had fled, only to turn up a short time later at a hospital, and that's where Huntsville police found him, with at least one hole in the leg.

As the saying goes, "when seconds count, police are minutes away," and although cops and sheriffs' deputies try to do a good job, they can't be on the scene when a crime goes down. Indeed, that's a rare event.

Good Samaritan v. Bad Behavior

Elsewhere in Alabama—Mobile to be exact— being the proverbial "Good Samaritan" with a gun didn't work out quite so well as it did for the Huntsville hero security guard.

When an armed private citizen intervened in the robbery of a Family Dollar Store, the young fellow on the receiving end of a bullet ended up receiving support from his family, as they contended the person who shot him during what was called an attempted robbery should have "just left the store," according to WALA, a Fox News affiliate.

That sort of thing happens occasionally, with family members complaining that their wounded or dead relative was "just beginning to turn his life around."

In this case, an 18-year-old identified as Adric White reportedly had a store employee on his knees with a gun aimed at the worker's head. That's what the armed citizen told investigators.

He reportedly saw the robbery unfolding and drew his gun, telling the masked suspect "don't move." But White allegedly did move, apparently swinging his gun around on the armed citizen, who fired.

WALA said one of the suspect's relatives contended, "If his (the customer's) life was not in danger, if no one had a gun up to him, if no one pointed a gun at him, what gives him the right to think that it's okay to just shoot someone?"

But in such cases, when an armed citizen concludes there is imminent danger of grave bodily harm or death, leaving is an option that may not be on the table.

There is an interesting angle to this story, according to the station. The story noted, "Court records show that White was out on bond for robbing The Original Oyster House at gunpoint a little more than a month before the Family Dollar robbery."

Of all the defensive gun uses found while researching this book, perhaps none so better addresses the wrongful "vigilante" impression than an incident in Florida at a "back to school" picnic event at a Titusville park than one involving a legally-armed citizen who was in the right place at the right time to intervene.

This incident made national news because of its unusual and heroic, albeit alarming nature. According to published reports, what began as a fistfight turned into a shootout that sent some 100 youngsters and adults scrambling for safety.

The two initial combatants were trading blows when one man departed from the Issac Campbell Park but returned a few minutes later, armed with a gun. He opened fire.

But in the crowd was the armed citizen, and he shot the gunman. Deputy Chief Todd Hutchinson was quoted stating, "We are extremely grateful that nobody else was injured in this incident."

The armed citizen did the right thing by remaining at the scene to talk with responding officers and cooperate with the investigation. One official told reporters that the armed bystander acted "within the law based on the preliminary investigation."

Partial credit for the outcome would go to Florida's controversial stand-your-ground law under which the armed Samaritan was able to act and essentially assume the role of first responder.

But he was not a "vigilante" in the dour sense, and he did not "take the law into his own hands." The law was there already for him to act.

7: 'GUN FREE ZONE' IS A DANGEROUS MYTH

Nothing so vividly illustrates the delusional state of the gun prohibitionist's mindset than the stubborn defense of the so-called "gun-free school zone."

Repeated failures of that designation read like a history of mass shootings on school campuses. Columbine High School. Sandy Hook Elementary. Marjory Stoneman Douglas High School. Santa Fe High School. Marysville-Pilchuck High School. Arapaho High School. STEM school at Highlands Ranch.

Each of these and similar incidents represent the abysmal failure of a gun control law adopted with high expectations, great promise and no small amount of empty rhetoric aimed at convincing the voters back home in the suburbs that "something" was being done to make their children safe. The result was words on paper, and they do not make a very effective barrier against an individual determined to cause harm to defenseless students and staff.

According to information published by the Second Amendment Foundation (SAF) based on research done by the Crime Prevention Research Center (CPRC), "Most gunmen are smart enough to know that they can kill more people if they attack places where victims can't defend themselves; 98 percent of mass public shootings since 1950 have occurred in places where citizens are banned from having guns.

"In Europe," the Foundation noted, "every mass public shooting in history has occurred in a gun-free zone. And, Europe is no stranger to mass public shootings. In the past eight years, it has experienced a per-capita casualty rate 50 percent higher than that of the U.S."

Following the horrible shooting at Sandy Hook, when gun rights organizations declared that the only thing that stops a bad guy with a gun is a good guy with a gun, this truth has been demonstrated repeatedly, and each time it happens, anti-gunners routinely ignore it.

At the Santa Fe High School shooting in Texas, the shooter was confronted by armed police officers and ultimately was taken into custody.

Sandy Hook killer Adam Lanza took his own life as police officers began arriving at the school.

Arapahoe High School gunman Karl Pierson took his own life as an armed sheriff's deputy, acting as the school's resource officer, rushed to the school library area where Pierson had opened fire.

Austin Wyatt Rollins shot himself in the head as a sheriff's deputy shot him in the hand, thus ending the attack at Great Mills High School in Maryland. He killed one other student and wounded a second victim before being confronted by Deputy Blaine Gaskill.

When Luke Woodham, the shooter at Pearl High School in Pearl, Mississippi was confronted by armed vice principal Joel Myrick, Woodham surrendered.

The list goes on, but the pattern seems to remain constant. When confronted by an armed person, school shooters either surrender or take their own lives.

Into this controversial political minefield came Trump Administration Education Secretary Betsy DeVos, who found herself accused of advocating the use of federal education funds to arm school teachers. The assertions were false, but the political tempest that erupted underscored the fanaticism of gun-free school advocates who also seem content to leave teachers and students far less protected than members of Congress and state legislatures.

What apparently ignited the fireworks was a story in the *New York Times* that suggested the Department of Education was actually considering the possibility of arming teachers, as noted by *USA Today* at the time. It didn't help when an Education Department press spokesperson issued a terse statement that said the agency was "constantly considering and evaluating policy issues, particularly related to school safety."

That was apparently enough to create the uproar. Perennially anti-gun-rights California Sen. Dianne Feinstein was quoted by *USA Today* alleging, "The goal of this policy is to pad the pockets of gun manufacturers and the gun lobby, not protect our children."

But the controversy raged without much, if any, attention to the fact that there are programs that offer training to volunteer teachers and/or school administrators in school districts that have adopted policies to allow armed staff on campus. The more typical scenario involves off- or even on-duty police or sheriff's deputies serving as "school resource officers." As noted earlier, there have been incidents in which these resource officers intervened to limit the mayhem.

The one standout exception was at Marjory Stoneman Douglas in Parkland, Fla. There, school security cameras captured a sheriff's deputy waiting outside a school building during the shooting that left 17 students and adults dead.

The FASTER program (for Faculty/ Administrator Safety Training & Emergency Response) was started in Ohio with participation from the Buckeye Firearms Association, parents, nationally-recognized safety and medical experts, and law enforcement. The program covers lots of ground, not only how to respond to the immediate threat of school violence, but what to do in the aftermath. At least 2,000 people have taken the course, according to an article that appeared in *GQ* titled "When You Give a Teacher a Gun." Writer Jay Willis took readers through the training course and dug into the mindset that guides teachers and school administrators to seek the training and take responsibility as a possible "first responder."

That does not appear to be the point, however, among opponents of armed teacher programs. Adherence to a "gun free zone" philosophy, even when it has been demonstrated repeatedly that school shooters are not deterred, outweighs any other consideration. It is almost like a religion in which faith in the "gun-free" designation overcomes the common sense of experience. Forget the fact that such designations have failed in the past, someday the signs will work.

There are rational arguments on both sides of the issue, of course, but they are often overshadowed by the irrational. Opponents have frequently asserted that an armed teacher might somehow be involved in an accidental shooting. Their guns might be stolen and used by a student. Teachers have enough to keep them busy during a school day, so adding the burden of being a first responder in an emergency only adds to their emotional workload. All of these arguments have been used to oppose any proposal that would allow teachers or administrators to voluntarily participate in such a program.

Proponents note that no gun belonging to an armed teacher or administrator has ever been involved in an accident. Those staffers with firearms are extremely careful to retain control of that gun throughout the school day, and they do it discreetly. Teachers or administrators who volunteer for this additional responsibility and the training that goes along with it know exactly what they're getting into. As the *GQ* article detailed, this is no lark for the participants. They look at FASTER program participation as a serious commitment, with a full understanding that lives—including their own—could be at stake in the event of an emergency.

Doomed to Failure

Designating some area as a "gun-free zone" is doomed to failure for the reason noted earlier. That doesn't just apply to schools. There are shopping malls, movie theaters, churches, other private businesses and public areas where guns are prohibited by local or state statutes, and where shootings have occurred; a theater in Aurora, Co., the Trolley Square Mall in Salt Lake City, the Oak Park Mall in Kansas City and the Tree of Life Synagogue in Pittsburgh are all good examples, and they are certainly not the only examples.

Indeed, the expectation that designating some area as a "gun-free zone" will prevent a tragedy almost falls within the generic standard of insanity: doing the same thing over and over, and expecting a different outcome. It cannot be repeated often enough: People determined to kill will ignore gun-free designations.

Why the gun prohibition movement doesn't get this has confounded Second Amendment activists for many years.

As noted by SAF in its messaging, "The evidence shows that gun-free zones are not the answer. Truth is, they are an added danger because they prevent legally-armed citizens from defending themselves and their neighbors."

SAF maintains that it is "time to get rid of gun-free zones."

"The U.S. has tried them for more than 20 years," SAF contended, "and evidence shows that gun-free zones actually increase the danger. Nobody wants to be a sitting duck in a maniac's shooting gallery."

Perhaps it is not that anti-gunners don't understand it so much as they simply refuse to accept the reality that they are completely wrong on this issue. Gun control proponents are more inclined to recommend additional restrictions when someone turns a gun-free zone into a killing field, rather than acknowledge that posting a sign on a door provided a false sense of security to the victims of a shooting.

Either that, or they simply don't care. As author Alan Gottlieb noted in an Op-Ed he submitted to *USA Today* following the mass shooting in Virginia Beach, Va., in 2019, "But the predictable knee-jerk reflex of the gun control crowd is to seek tighter restrictions on millions of people who harmed nobody, just to advance their agenda of public disarmament. That's not justice, it's social bigotry suggested by people who would never tolerate a similar broad brush policy were it aimed at the rights of any other social, religious or ethnic group."

There are some exceptions, such as the Trolley Square shooting. Killer Sulejman Talovic opened fire with a shotgun, killing five people. He was confronted by an armed off-duty police officer, Kenneth Hammond, from a nearby jurisdiction. He was joined by Salt Lake City Police Sgt. Andrew Oblad, and both engaged the gunman, who was subsequently killed a responding SWAT team.

Good guys with guns stopped a bad guy with a gun. Had those good guys not been present, it seems undeniable that Talovic would have continued his rampage.

At the time of the incident, author and researcher John Lott, founder and president of the Crime Prevention Research Center, published an image of a sign in the door of the mall that said weapons are not allowed inside the facility. That fact was overlooked by mainstream media, but it was seen by millions of Americans via social media.

Still, gun free zones are dangerous. They are where the vast majority of mass shootings occur, leaving the gun control crowd free to demand more gun restrictions for law-abiding citizens who had nothing at all to do with the crime.

In the Workplace

A few years ago, firearms instructor and gun writer Chuck Klein authored a book called *Guns in the Workplace* that explained the concept of employees bringing firearms to the job. Klein discussed such issues as general business policy, crisis control, possessing firearms on company property, disciplinary procedures, the use of lethal force and more.

Three paragraphs in the first chapter should catch everyone's attention:

"When a business posts their private property they, obviously, are directing this prohibition to those who are legally permitted to carry concealed firearms. Those carrying a firearm without a license are criminals and thus, by their very definition, don't comply with signs, laws or other rules.

"Companies compensate their employees with a host of 'security' devices such as surveillance cameras, lots of light, direct lines to alarm companies, and other bells and whistles. But, most of these 'security' measures only provide AFTER-THE-FACT protection. In other words, none of these reactive tools are of any value when the shooting is about to begin.

"When an employer restricts the carrying of legal firearms upon his premise by legally licensed persons, he does NOT create a Gun Free Zone. What he establishes, sans other protective measures, is a Self-Defense Free Zone."

A case in Oregon underscores the fact that discrimination against gun owners, even those defending themselves and their employers from harm, has a habit of hurting the wrong people. In this case, the victim of corporate policy and political correctness was the convenience store clerk who drew a legally-concealed handgun on a would-be armed robber who pulled a hatchet.

Displaying any kind of weapon during a robbery is the easiest way to enhance a criminal sentence upon conviction. Robbers seem to know this and evidently most don't seem to care because they seem also to realize that getting caught is not guaranteed.

The story in Oregon involved a clerk at a Plaid Pantry store, which has a no-weapons policy for its employees. But when someone is threatening you with a hatchet, store policy took a backseat for the clerk, who did lose his job over the incident. That's certainly better than losing one's life.

The robber got away, too, so he'll probably try again until he gets caught or shot.

Plaid Pantry at the time of the incident issued a statement that would not be terribly reassuring to anyone applying for a job on the graveyard (overnight) shift:

"Plaid Pantry adheres to proven industry best-practices, including the policy of no weapons in the store. The Company makes significant investments in security equipment and training in robbery deterrence and violence prevention. All employees are trained in these procedures and receive ongoing refresher training. In the event a robbery does occur, the focus shifts entirely to non-resistance, cooperation, and violence avoidance for the safety of our employees and customers."

Yes, but what about the employee who gets physically assaulted even when they do cooperate? Non-resistance, cooperation and violence avoidance may sound great in a statement to the press but it doesn't go very far in an emergency room or at a memorial service, and to be honest, this "proven industry best-practice" standard has been equally proven to be a total failure when it comes to preventing the murder of a clerk in, say, a convenience store.

The now-former Plaid Pantry employee, Kristofer Follis, told reporters that he "knew" his job was finished as soon as he drew his legally-carried sidearm. The would-be robber momentarily dropped to his knees and put up his hands. But then he jumped up and fled. Notice that he was not shot in the back by the armed store clerk.

Maybe the lesson in this story is what Follis told KOIN News. He would do it again.

There Was a Doctor in the House

One thing that distinguishes self-defense shootings from criminal misuse of firearms is that in the aftermath, the media gives any news coverage of such an event a very short duration; that is, the story is not reported much longer than 24 hours if even that.

Typically, the reporting remains local as well. Such incidents do not receive the same degree of national news coverage, if they get any at all, that is frequently given to a mass shooting where there were no "good guys with guns" to intervene, until police arrive.

The gun prohibition lobby invariably goes absolutely silent. No gun control organization has ever celebrated the act of an armed private citizen to defend unarmed people from violent attack. It is as though some force had suddenly robbed them of their vocal cords, and keep them uninformed about the heroic intervention of an armed private citizen.

One significant case in point was an incident that occurred at a hospital near Philadelphia, Pa. one summer afternoon, involving a psychiatrist who happened to be armed, and a man named Richard Plotts, who entered the Mercy Wellness Center with evil intent.

Plotts was described as a man with "a history of unspecified psychiatric problems." He had served time in prison, making him ineligible to possess a firearm. He'd actually violated his parole some years earlier for firearm possession, according to an NBC News account. Add to that background the murder of a caseworker and it pretty well sums up this fellow's life.

Arriving at the doctor's office with his caseworker, Plotts reportedly got into an argument with the doctor and caseworker, and the situation deteriorated almost immediately. Before it was over, Plotts killed the caseworker and was subsequently shot by the physician, Dr. Lee Silverman, using his personally-owned sidearm. Silverman didn't escape injury, however. He was grazed in the head by a bullet, so it is clear Plotts intended to kill him, and possibly as many other people as he could. The gunman was hit more than once and then wrestled to the ground by another doctor and caseworker, according to an account that appeared in *USA Today*.

Plotts was Silverman's patient, which would certainly give him insight into what sort of fellow he was dealing with.

It should be noted that at the time, *USA Today* reported the wellness center had a sign posted at the entrance that visitors had to check their guns. Plotts obviously ignored that sign, which underscores the futility of expecting a piece of paper, cardboard or plastic to make much of an impression on anyone planning a violent act in a gun-free zone.

Then Came Virginia Beach

The debate over gun control heated up swiftly in the aftermath of the lone-gunman attack in a municipal building in Virginia Beach, Va.

While any private citizen licensed to carry in the Commonwealth can bring a gun into a public building, employees aren't supposed to walk in and open fire, killing a dozen people. That's what happened when a man identified as DeWayne Craddock, a civil engineer with 15 years on the job, brought two handguns into the workplace hours after reportedly submitting his resignation.

For the record, this was a "gun-free zone."

Nothing could more clearly illustrate the weakness of the "gun-free zone" argument than this attack, and quite possibly nothing better defines the exploitive nature of gun control extremism than the reaction by anti-gun Democrat Virginia Gov. Ralph Northam. The attack happened on a Friday, and the following Tuesday, Northam showed up at Virginia Beach followed by the news media, to announce his proposed "gun reform" package. It was nothing but warmed over gun control from previous efforts, and the Citizens Committee for the Right to Keep and Bear Arms immediately threw down the gauntlet.

Northam vowed to seek so-called "universal background checks" and bans on so-called "assault weapons" and suppressors. He would push for extreme risk protective orders, child access prevention and other restrictions that included reinstating the Commonwealth's one-handgun-a-month restriction and requiring people to report lost or stolen firearms.

But CCRKBA, in a scathing news release, challenged, "The killer in Virginia Beach had already passed multiple background checks, including an enhanced check to legally purchase a suppressor. The incident didn't involve a so-called 'assault weapon,' but two handguns. There was no indication that the gunman was an extreme risk to anybody, and this awful event didn't involve a child gaining access to any firearm.

"So tell us, Ralph," the gun rights group demanded, "just what part of your extremist gun control wish list do you think would have prevented what happened in Virginia Beach?"

Indeed, according to several Northam critics, nothing in his proposals would have prevented the shooting, had they been in effect at the time.

Not surprisingly, the governor did not respond to CCRKBA's question, nor did the mainstream press prod Northam to answer.

"Northam has dusted off the same ragged old gun prohibition agenda," CCRKBA said. "None of the things he wants would have made even the slightest difference, and he knows it."

Adding to the fireworks, Virginia House of Delegates Speaker Kirk Cox issued a statement that also essentially rejected Northam's anti-gun grandstanding. Instead, Cox proposed legislation that would hold criminals accountable for their misdeeds while leaving law-abiding gun owners alone.

"We believe addressing gun violence starts with holding criminals accountable for their actions," Cox said at the time, "not infringing on the constitutional rights of law-abiding citizens."

In the process of murdering a dozen people—which happens to be against the law anywhere in the United States—the Virginia Beach killer ignored a law against bringing a suppressor into the city, where they are reportedly prohibited.

So much for the myth that a "gun-free zone" designation is going to keep anybody safe, especially from a determined individual who is intent to commit mayhem.

The uncomfortable truth about Virginia Beach and similar horrors—the truth around which the gun prohibition lobby and anti-gun politicians such as Northam reflexively dance—is that no law on the books now, or that has been proposed, would have prevented the Virginia Beach tragedy.

What might have changed the situation, of course, would have been a legally-armed employee who was able to fire back. But as explained earlier with the quote from Chuck Klein in his book about guns in the workplace, the "gun-free zone" is a "self-defense free zone" where the armed employee is simply not going to materialize.

A 'Big Lie'

Longtime Second Amendment legal scholar and attorney David Hardy authored a short but salient book titled *Mass Killings – Myth, Reality, and Solutions*, in which he quickly took to task the perennial claim by gun prohibitionists that mass shootings only happen in the United States.

"In 2015," Hardy wrote in the first chapter, "(then) President Obama gave voice to this understanding: 'We have a pattern now of mass shootings in this country that has no parallel anywhere else in the world.' In an address to the nation the following year, he remarked, 'I say this every time we've got one of these mass shootings. This just doesn't happen in other countries.'

"Actually," Hardy continued, "it does. The record death toll from a mass shooting came in Norway, in 2011: 67 deaths. The record death toll from a mass killing of any type came in China, in 2001; the killer used bombs to take 108 lives. In 1982 a berserk South Korean policeman killed 56 (the same number that died in our worst shooting, in Las Vegas), in 2007 two Ukrainians killed 25 with a hammer and a pipe, in 1986 a Columbian used a six-shot revolver to kill 29 in a Bogota restaurant."

Hardy went on to remind readers that the worst school mass slaying and the only use of a firearm by the perpetrator, school board member Andrew Kehoe, was to fire a shot from a bolt-action Model 54 Winchester rifle that set off a cache of explosives. That happened to the school in Bath, Michigan in 1927, and 44 lives were taken when Kehoe blew up the school building.

According to a detailed account by the Smithsonian, Kehoe murdered his wife, Nellie, their two horses and burned their farmhouse. Investigators found a sign on the fence that said, "Criminals are made, not born."

It should be noted that Obama has made a habit of spreading myths about Americans and firearms. He was taken to task for remarks made at a conference in Sao Paulo, Brazil in which he asserted to the audience, "Gun laws in the United States don't make much sense. Anybody can buy any weapon, anytime without, you know, without much if any regulation. They can buy over the Internet. They can buy machine guns."

That comment was declared "mostly false" by PolitiFact a few days later. Writing at *National Review*, Charles C.S. Cooke accused Obama of being "misleading" in his comments. Almost simultaneously writing at P.J. Media, nationally-syndicated talk host Dennis Prager asserted that Obama "fabricated a series of falsehoods" and further complained that the silence of the American news media about these canards speaks to the media's lack of character.

But Obama habitually gets away with this sort of rhetoric because he became a media darling during his tenure in the White House that some people consider disastrous or at least scandal-plagued.

Likewise, leading national gun prohibitionists frequently mouth the same dishonest rhetoric and are rarely challenged by reporters. Many believe this is the primary reason why so many in the firearms community consider "mainstream" journalists to be untrustworthy and their reportage to be unreliable if not totally false.

In his book, Hardy discusses a number of "myths" about mass killers. He declared false the assertion that mass or school shootings are increasing and he also concluded that mass killers are not necessarily he victims of bullies, or that they "just snapped."

There is only one part of Obama's Brazil remarks with which typical Second Amendment activists could agree, and that's where the ex-president asserted that U.S. gun laws don't make sense. Ask any veteran gun rights advocate and they will immediately concur, because as gun laws change from one jurisdiction to another, they are frequently in conflict and often completely contradictory.

Intellectual Honesty

Would it be wrong to consider arguments in favor of "gun-free zones" and against concealed carry to be intellectually dishonest?

After all, the overwhelming majority of mass shootings seem to occur in "gun-free zones" where the victims are essentially denied the tools to defend themselves.

In an opinion piece written for the *Washington Post* and syndicated to several other newspapers, Lott, of the Crime Prevention Research Center, observed that "98 percent of mass public shootings since 1950 have occurred in places where citizens are banned from having guns."

He also said something that reinforces what was covered in an earlier chapter.

"The national media tend to ignore case after case of mass public shootings being stopped by armed private citizens." Why the bias?

Could it be that the "national media" Lott mentions is overwhelmingly anti-gun itself, and that there is a conscious effort to downplay the legal defensive use of firearms, so as to not give the public any idea about the effectiveness of fighting back?

In his article, Lott listed several places where shootings had occurred in so-called "gun-free zones." The problem with all of these places is that killers evidently don't read signs on doors, or didn't get the memo about not opening fire in a gun-free area. There was the Borderline Bar & Grill in California, Chicago's Mercy Hospital & Medical Center, plus the Westroads Mall in Omaha, the Tacoma Mall in Washington; all places that guns are not supposed to be carried.

So, when California Gov. Gavin Newsom claims, "This doesn't happen anywhere else on the planet," and anti-gun New York Congresswoman Carolyn Maloney contends, "We stand alone in the world in the number of mass shootings," Lott suggests there might be a credibility problem.

Lott then looked at several places around the globe that appear to leave U.S. mass shootings in the dust, including the Las Vegas attack, amplifying the points that author/attorney Hardy made with his book on mass shooting myths.

And while we are on the subject of intellectual honesty, it seems to be a frequent reaction from gun control organizations to be absolutely silent in the wake of an armed citizen intervention in what might have been a tragedy, but wasn't.

As we have discussed earlier, and will continue discussing in the remaining chapters, the gradually increasing instances of "good guys with guns" taking action essentially as reluctant first responders are met with stone silence from the anti-self-defense lobby. Whatever else gun control activists might be, by advocating for the disarmament of private citizens, they are perhaps unintentionally arguing against self-defense.

Only in cases where they might be able to get away with condescension will anti-gunners dare open their mouths following an incident in which an armed citizen takes a decisive action that saves lives.

One gun control advocate in Illinois had just such a reaction following the incident in Cicero discussed in Chapter Four.

Colleen Daley, executive director of the Illinois Council Against Handgun Violence, was quoted by the *Chicago Tribune*.

"This situation worked out OK, but what if it hadn't?" she reportedly said. "It easily could have gone the other way. To sit here and say that concealed carry is the answer to all of our gun violence problems, or more, that armed people are going to keep us safer, that's not true."

Well, police are armed, and at last check they were people, so it appears Daley is at least suggesting that armed police don't keep the public safer.

And on the subject of intellectual honesty, what about the gun control proponent who refuses to post his or her residence as gun-free? One often sees this discussed on social media, where people at both ends of the scale argue about whether the anti-gunner is being dishonest by not posting a sign that says "There are no guns in this home."

Would refusing to do this amount to an unintentional admission by the anti-gunner that he/she really does not believe such signs prevent violent crime from happening inside? It's a question one should pose to an anti-gunner at any Town Hall event, and if they attempt to dismiss it as irrelevant, they should be called on it politely but firmly.

Writing at *Knox News*, author/researcher Lott had this observation: "These killers might be crazy, but they aren't stupid. Picking defenseless targets means being able to kill more people. A long list of killers explicitly have stated this reasoning, including the 2015 Charleston, S.C., church shooting, the 2012 theater shooting in Aurora, Colo., and the 2015 attack in San Bernardino, Calif."

And he concluded the article thusly: "Gun-free zones are magnets for murderers. Even the most ardent gun-control advocate…would never put 'Gun-

Free Zone' signs on his home. Let's stop putting them elsewhere.

It's much the same double standard situation one finds when opponents of a border wall, for example, live in private residences surrounded by walls, or live in gated communities with walls around the entire tract.

The double standard is inescapable.

On the other hand, gun rights advocates occasionally display decals on their doors or windows that warn would-be home invaders that the owner of the property is armed and that there is nothing inside worth risking one's life for. Some might interpret that as a threat, or as a signal to burglars to break in when nobody is home because there may be guns inside.

The happy medium is to not post any signs at all.

Don't Go There

It probably will come as no surprise that many self-defense activists will not patronize businesses that post "no guns allowed" signs, or decals showing a silhouette of a firearm with the universally-recognized circled cross-out emblazoned over it.

Some years ago in Seattle, there was a concerted effort launched by a gun control organization to enlist local businesses to post their establishments against firearms. Other businesses in other cities have done likewise, and one can find references occasionally on social media or gun-related forums from people who simply have refrained from doing business with them.

After all, nobody is required to patronize any business that makes one feel unwelcome.

In his aforementioned book about mass killings, Hardy notes near the end, "We know that mass shooters consider security in choosing a target." Since it is alleged that most mass shootings occur in so-called "gun-free zones," it would seem logical that signs identifying such places might attract the attention of some publicity-seeking person looking to become immortalized by an evil act.

In the aftermath of the theater shooting in Aurora, Colorado, it was reported that the theater in question was the only one in that area posted against carrying firearms inside.

If it is indeed true that the would-be mass killer scouts his targets looking for soft ones, perhaps businesses would be wiser to not advertise themselves as "gun-free" and leave the social justice war to others.

It is up to each person to be ultimately responsible for his or her own safety, and make a decision on whether to patronize a place that might prevent fighting back in the event that becomes necessary.

While law enforcement does try to respond quickly to life-threatening situations, more often than not responding officers or deputies arrive after the fact. In those cases, the armed citizen becomes his or her own "first responder" as the cases discussed in this chapter illustrate.

8: 'NO CHARGES WILL BE FILED'

Certainly, the best news for an armed private citizen who has had to act in self-defense, or in defense of another innocent party, is that they will not face criminal prosecution for essentially having been the intended victim of a crime, but successfully fought back.

Bad enough that one should be victimized by a criminal or crazy person, but the emotional impact is definitely compounded by having some over-zealous prosecutor file criminal charges to judge your conduct in a split-second emergency when they have the luxury of hindsight and no immediate threat.

Many stories about good guys with guns will include the notation that the armed citizen "will not face charges, authorities said." One often hears complaints about police officers "getting away with murder," but when the proverbial shoe is on the other foot and it is the private citizen who has had to act in order to save his or her life, or the life of a child, parent, neighbor or friend, the word "murder" probably is not part of the conversation.

But don't make the false presumption that every time someone shoots and claims self-defense, it's a free walk. Generically speaking, the armed citizen must be in genuine fear of grave bodily harm or death. Self-defense and use-of-force statutes vary from state to state. What may be perfectly legal in Florida or Louisiana may get you in trouble somewhere else, say Massachusetts or New Jersey.

It is incumbent upon the armed private citizen to know and understand the self-defense laws in his or her state, and more importantly, have attorneys and investigators who understand the law as well.

All of that said, there are cases of armed self-defense which are so clearly justified that the result of an investigation falls well-within the generic description of "clear cut."

Indeed, that's essentially how one local police administrator described it. Leavenworth Police Major Dan Nicodemus was quoted by KTLA observing that the case was "pretty cut and dried," and even the family of the dead man told reporters they held no grudge against the elderly would-be victim.

The woman who fired that shot subsequently suffered a heart attack as the crime scene investigation was in progress and had to be transported to a local hospital.

As the story unfolded, it was learned that the woman's home had been the scene of an attempted burglary about one week before, and that she had "obtained a .22-caliber handgun" that she kept in the bedroom while she was sleeping.

Looking into the background of the man she shot, it was revealed that Ralph Byrd Jr., had a history of drug abuse resulting from the breakup of a marriage and the death of a "father figure." But his brother, Elvis was quoted in news reports noting that drugs "controlled him."

"They took him over," he said, "and that is all he cared about. He would do anything he had to do to get high."

A case in Covington, Kentucky that left one man dead and a couple of accomplices on the run ended pretty much the same way, with no charges against the son of a homeowner, who pulled the trigger.

The late-night home invasion at the home of Floyd and Darlene Gillie certainly didn't end the way a man identified as 43-year-old Joshua Kersey apparently planned. Instead of learning the whereabouts of someone who hadn't lived in the home for several years—which was ostensibly the reason they broke in—Kersey wound up with a fatal gunshot wound to the chest and his cohorts fled into the night. Responding police officers found him on the ground outside the Gillie home and he was armed.

The Gillies' 24-year-old son, Floyd, Jr., grabbed a gun when the commotion started and fired as Kersey and the other two reportedly approached his bedroom.

According to the *River City News,* Kenton County Commonwealth's Attorney Rob Sanders said no charges would be filed, noting, "Mr. Gillie was justifiably in fear for his safety and the safety of his parents, so he was entitled to use deadly force in defense of their home."

Kentucky has a "Castle Doctrine" law and that played a major part in the outcome of the investigation. Prosecutor Sanders declared that "This wasn't a close call; it was clearly justified."

In another case in Clayton County, Georgia, a homeowner fatally shot an 18-year-old suspect who was allegedly trying to break into the house. When police arrived, they found the wounded teen lying at the foot of the outside steps. He died en route to the hospital, according to the new report from "11 Live" news.

The news agency quoted Maj. Anthony Thuman with the Clayton County Police, who observed, "People have the right to defend themselves. That's the point we want to drive home. You have the right to defend yourself."

As it turned out, the dead teen had "several run-ins" with local police as a juvenile.

Deflating Value of Armed Citizens

Despite repeated anecdotal examples of armed citizens justifiably using force to stop or prevent crimes and harm to the innocent, there are efforts to downplay their importance and even belittle the notion of fighting back.

In a publication called *The Conversation*, an article headlined "How the good guy with a gun became a deadly American fantasy" took issue with the slogan that "the only way to stop a bad guy with a gun is a good guy with a gun."

The article focused on the premise that the "good guy with a gun" is essentially a myth that was born with stories about "a certain type of protagonist" that began with "American crime fiction."

Apparently attempting to rain on everyone's parade, the writer contends, "The problem with this archetype is that it's just that: an archetype. A fictional fantasy."

Except that there is nothing fictional about the armed citizens mentioned here and in previous chapters, who have fought back and survived. None of these people makes a habit of bragging about their deeds, since the taking of a human life can hardly be the most pleasant thing anyone could ever do. But their use of lethal force toward a good end should not be so casually dismissed, as is habitually done by self-defense opponents. Many, if not most, times there is a sound defense with a firearm, the gun control crowd ignores it, hoping the story goes away swiftly.

When a man armed with a knife repeatedly stabbed a 25-year-old Chicago woman one autumn afternoon in what appeared to be a case of self-defense in relation to a domestic incident, the woman had a gun and she used it. The man she shot was identified as Pleasure Cardell Singleton Jr., and he succumbed to his wounds.

The *Chicago Sun-Times* reported that police determined the woman in this case had acted in self-defense and no charges were filed.

This might be alluded to as a case of someone bringing a knife to a gunfight, and such situations often end badly for the person armed with a knife. The fact that the woman was wounded several times underscores her fear of grave bodily harm or death, and she was in serious condition at the time she was transported to the hospital.

But some stories manage to take on lives of their own. One example from Washington State seems to linger as a text book case of road rage going completely bad.

A young woman identified as Aubrey Bowlin was riding a motorcycle southbound on Interstate 5 near the town of Milton. She had a confrontation with a 60-year-old motorist who physically assaulted her when they stopped alongside the highway. Fearing for her life, Bowlin drew a legally-carried sidearm and shot Bruce W. Jones that fateful day.

She had acted in self-defense under the Washington statute, which still ranks as one of the best use-of-force laws in the country for its clarity and directness. Following an investigation, the Pierce

County Prosecutor's office concluded that Bowlin did fire in self-defense and that translated to no charges filed.

So, why would anyone wish to downplay the difference that having a firearm made to the 24-year-old Bowlin? Again, the silence from gun prohibitionist lobbying organizations or even individual anti-gunners is deafening following justifiable self-defense incidents. It doesn't support their narrative, that's why.

What about Carjackers?

We've discussed a couple of carjacking cases in previous chapters, but there is no universal rule on this situation. In some states, shooting a carjacker might land you in prison, and at the very least, a courtroom. At other times, however, circumstances often make it an open-and-shut case.

The *Palm Beach Post* reported on one such incident when a man identified as Terrence Wilson Jr., was fatally shot by an unidentified car owner when he tried to take the vehicle. In this case, the man's 5-year-old daughter was seated in the vehicle.

The incident happened in Lake Park and the Palm Beach County Sheriff's Office told the *Palm Beach Post* that no charges would be filed in the case.

Wilson's background was not that of a model citizen, either. In the aftermath of the case, the newspaper reported that he had been arrested in Palm Beach County twice between 2016 and the time he was killed. He was convicted of burglary in May 2016, and that was for breaking into a car. The following November, he "allegedly failed" to appear in court for driving without a license.

Of course, the armed citizen who shot Wilson likely didn't know anything about his record, but he did know that Wilson was attempting to make off with a car in which his daughter was seated.

Under most circumstances, shooting a carjacker is a dicey legal proposition, but that's obviously not a hard and fast rule. A child in the car, or an armed carjacker who threatens to harm the driver, perhaps a shot fired or an attempt to physically harm the person whose car is being jacked can all tilt the situation in favor of the armed citizen.

Recall the Washington Walmart parking lot incident discussed in Chapter One, in which a legally-armed citizen fatally shot a would-be carjacker who had just seriously wounded the car's driver. In a rampage situation like that, when harm has been visibly done in one's presence and any reasonable person might react in the same way, the "good guy (or girl) with a gun" will more likely be acting within the parameters of the state use-of-force laws, but it's a good idea to check those statutes to be absolutely certain.

There was an incident in downtown Chicago involving a legally-armed private citizen who, according to WGN News, also did not face any charges after he fatally shot a would-be carjacker. This was no minor caper, either. The 41-year-old armed citizen was driving a BMW when he was rear-ended by a younger man driving a Volkswagen at about 3 a.m. one morning.

When the BMW owner got out of his car, according to WGN, he was confronted by the 22-year-old who was armed, and demanded his keys to the BMW. Much to his short-lived surprise, the older man, who was not identified by news agencies, drew his legally-carried sidearm and promptly shot the would-be thief.

This case also concluded with no charges against the armed citizen, as it was clearly self-defense.

A suspected multiple carjacker was fatally wounded in Florida's Hillsborough County after he reportedly tried to jack several cars, according to a local ABC News affiliate.

The dead man was identified as Eric Jackson, who reportedly was armed with a pistol as he strolled around a Publix parking lot, apparently looking for victims. When a supervisor at a local business went to check his own car, Jackson reportedly approached and there was a confrontation that ended in multiple shots.

In this case, WFTS News reported that no charges had been filed, adding that the dead man had an extensive drug-related record.

Do some Homework

Here's a challenge. Using your favorite Internet search engine, type in the words "No charges were filed" and see what happens. When the authors did this as part of our research, using Google we were advised that there were 925 *million* results.

Or try "No charges filed in shooting" and one will find a more modest 30 *million* references. Even considering that there will be a multitude of repeat reports dealing with the same incidents, you are still talking about millions of self-defense uses of firearms. Some of these cases are intriguing and involve armed private citizens, while many involve police officers shooting suspects.

One case that occurred in Craig, Colorado involved a man identified as Mario Cruz Vigil. The 60-year-old was fatally wounded after breaking into a house, armed with a gun. The homeowners shot him twice, once in the chest with a shotgun and then in the thigh with a .30-06-caliber rifle. It was the rifle bullet that fatally wounded the older man, who had a blood alcohol content of 0.132 according to the *Craig Daily Press*, nearly twice the legal limit.

At the time, the District Attorney noted that this was not only a case of self-defense, but it fell within the parameters of Colorado's stand-your-ground law protecting citizens who kill intruders, what critics have long called the "make my day" statute based on a line of dialogue in an old Clint Eastwood film, one of his "Dirty Harry" Callahan series.

In a more recent incident in Milwaukee, Wisconsin, no charges were filed in a shooting incident that was determined to be self-defense by the District Attorney's office. In this case, another 60-year-old man was apparently the aggressor, and he was shot in the leg by a 28-year-old woman.

What set this case apart was its location. According to the local Fox News affiliate, the shooting occurred "very near the Police Administration Building" in downtown Milwaukee. At least detectives didn't have to go very far to investigate.

This was a daylight shooting incident, and both combatants were armed. The man was carrying some sort of "metal object," but he made a near-fatal error in the victim selection process. What set this off was an argument that quickly escalated into something more dramatic.

At this point, armed citizens need to remind themselves repeatedly to always keep a cool head while carrying a defensive sidearm.

In Walhalla, S.C., authorities said the shooting death of a man identified as Angel Rodriguez Jr., was self-defense. He died in a Greenville hospital one day after having been shot by a 27-year-old man at an apartment complex.

As reported by the *Greenville News*, "Police said the shooting was self-defense. There will be no criminal charges brought against the other person involved, 27-year-old Eqequiel Rodriquez, police said."

Legal Support

For many years, the Second Amendment Foundation, based in Bellevue, Washington, has offered an attorney-referral service to people in need of qualified legal counsel. While SAF does not pay the legal bills, the ability to call this organization and be referred to one or more attorneys in their region can be invaluable.

The list of "resource" attorneys is frequently updated, and there is no fee for the referral.

One should never wait until the last minute to seek competent legal assistance, however.

Not all cases of self-defense wrap up so neatly as those mentioned in this chapter. One cannot always count on a quick resolution, especially if there is an aggressive prosecutor looking for a headline.

One might also consider joining organizations that provide education and assistance when it comes to the legal fallout of a self-defense incident.

Among these are the United States Concealed Carry Association, U.S. Law Shield and the Armed Citizens Legal Defense Network.

Armed private citizens, and there are millions of them as noted earlier, are invariably advised to seek competent instruction on the use of firearms and local self-defense laws. There are many programs available, including some specifically for women, and they have provided training for legions of good citizens who do not wish to make a bad mistake.

Be careful when dealing initially with public defenders, if an investigation goes that far. They may not always be up to speed on self-defense law, and you only get one chance to not keep yourself out of trouble.

Another possible avenue for armed citizens to find good legal support is in the newsletters of local gun rights organizations. Often pro-gun-rights attorneys will advertise in such publications, and they may offer both civil and criminal defense services.

Just because someone is cleared of any criminal wrongdoing in a self-defense shooting is no guarantee that the family of the person shot is going to forgo civil action. Civil lawsuits against armed citizens are nothing new, and there have been documented case of perpetrators or their families filing costly lawsuits against a good guy with a gun. Sadly, not all of those cases turn out well for the armed citizen.

Being in the right is no protection from being wronged in the civil courts, and remember always that the individual who is shot, no matter what sort of criminal past they may have, will frequently be described as a person who was "just beginning to turn his life around." In those cases, violent criminals miraculously become saints.

For information concerning legal representation for cases of armed self-defense, please check these websites as well as others:

- usconcealedcarry.com

- www.uslawshield.com

- armedcitizensnetwork.org

- SAF.org

9: TAKE IT FROM EXPERTS: TRAIN, LEARN

Among legally-armed private citizens are countless numbers of people who have taken their defense of self and others seriously enough to have attended one or more training "academies" in an effort to improve their defensive skills, and increase their understanding of the parameters of acceptable, justifiable use of force.

Naturally, some of these folks have had the misfortune to actually use those skills in life-or-death situations. The law of averages doesn't play favorites, and as the numbers of well-trained armed citizens increase, the odds of one or more such folks being involved in a self-defense incident increase exponentially.

The authors reached out to a handful of the professional trainers to get a perspective unique to the firearms culture. One is a retired sheriff and the other two retired from municipal law enforcement with a combined experience of scores of years.

Being in an armed confrontation does not play out like television with commercial breaks. People can get hurt, occasionally killed. We've spent the previous eight chapters discussing such cases. Now it's time to talk about how one can prepare for the day they hope never comes, when circumstances beyond one's control land an armed citizen in the middle of a storm.

Massad Ayoob is possibly one of the most famous self-defense firearms instructors and authorities on the map. He is an author, prolific writer and has appeared in court cases as an expert witness on self-defense issues. Years ago he founded and operated the Lethal Force Institute, and today he heads the Massad Ayoob Group, traveling the country teaching various levels of firearms and self-defense strategies. Years ago, he authored a book titled *In The Gravest Extreme – The Role of The Firearm in Personal Protection*. It became something of an overnight sensation and even today, decades after the first edition rolled off the press, the book is considered a classic.

He told the authors via email that people who come to his courses "want to be as competent and responsible as possible with their firearms, to keep themselves and their families safe from crime. They want a full understanding of the laws that allow them to protect themselves and their loved ones."

Likewise, Ken Campbell, chief operating officer at the world-famous Gunsite Academy near Paulden, Arizona explained why students attend courses at this facility, which was founded by the late Col. Jeff Cooper, considered by many to have been the "father of modern pistolcraft."

"The vast majority," Campbell observed, "want to become stronger in the gun handling and marksmanship so they can gain confidence to handle issues when they must face them. The 'Mindset' is what it crucial and it is enhanced once they have that learned confidence."

"Mindset?"

According to Cooper, the "combat mindset" is the most important "tool" one can possess in a gunfight. He wrote about it at length in *Principles of Personal Defense*, as noted in an online biography, and one can find references in some of his magazine articles, which frequently show up today in firearms periodicals.

Campbell quoted Cooper when asked what Gunsite students hope to achieve.

"Peace of mind of crisis management in interpersonal confrontation."

But Campbell didn't leave it there.

"I would hope they learn that their brain is the primary weapon and if they follow the 'Color Code' and 'Principles of Personal Defense' as Cooper offered them, avoidance. That is, be alert and aware and avoid the problem if you suspect it.

"If you can't avoid (a violent confrontation)," he continued, "your alertness should allow you to be prepared to face and properly handle most confrontations. Weapons handling and marksmanship are important, but mindset is the primary advantage."

Cooper's 'Color Code'

During his decades of teaching firearms skills, Gunsite founder Cooper established a simple, easy-to-remember color code to reflect alertness levels; that is, how aware someone is about their surroundings, possible dangers or threats, and whether their environment is safe or unsafe.

This color code has been taught by other instructors across the country, and it appears to have withstood the test of time. Legally-armed citizens should learn and understand this code. Here are Cooper's four "Condition levels"

WHITE: Essentially, you are in a state of ease with your situation and surroundings, even asleep. You are not paying attention to anything going on around you. The short translation is that your guard is down completely.

YELLOW: In "Condition Yellow," you are still in a relaxed state, but you are paying attention to your surroundings, including people in your immediate proximity. At this level of alertness, you should not be startled by anything that happens, including any action taken by anyone nearby.

ORANGE: This is, according to the code, a "heightened state of awareness" that there may be a possible danger. You are paying attention to something or someone who might pose a threat to your safety.

RED: In "Condition Red," it is basically "Game On." You're focused on the possible threat and prepared to act accordingly, if the threat unfolds and a reaction/response is required. At this point, you do not actually open fire, but you should be prepared to defend yourself.

Cooper's "color code" has become part of the lexicon among defensive trainers and a generation of legally-armed citizens who have taken advanced pistolcraft training.

Out in the Pacific Northwest, Marty Hayes, founder and CEO of the Firearms Academy of Seattle has similarly observed the desire among his students to learn the kind of skills and mindset that Cooper fostered decades ago.

"Many people," he commented, "are simply wanting to satisfy that basic need, not realizing that in order to potentially use the gun effectively to stop a criminal from attacking, (or stop him as he is attacking) that they need much more skill than simply the ability to hold and fire the gun safely and competently."

At FAS, Hayes detailed, "We explain that the armed citizen needs to be able to shoot just as good as a police officer who has had 80 hours of firearms training. After all, the armed citizen is facing the very same criminal element as the police do, but the armed citizen does it without body armor, police back-up, two way radios, etc. They typically face the criminal element alone, so their skills need to be top-notch. Otherwise, they are leaving their survival up to the skills of the criminal attacker."

This is why the mindset is paramount. Whether the armed citizen gets instruction from a local trainer or goes to one of the big national "shooting schools"—and there are several from which to choose—it is not just about learning to repeatedly punch holes in cardboard targets, but about absorbing knowledge that comes from the experience of people who have "been there and done that." They have held people at gunpoint, they have been to crime scenes and understand the dynamics of a self-defense shooting.

It was actually Cooper who created the four easily-remembered rules of firearm safety:

- All guns are always loaded.

- Never let the muzzle cover anything you are not willing to destroy

- Keep your finger off the trigger until your sights are on the target

- Identify your target and what is behind it

These were actually boiled down from the "Ten Commandments of Gun Safety," and they are always relevant. To see some of the very worst gun handling, watch prime time crime shows on television. Westerns, both on the small and big screens, are also sources of indigestion for experienced firearms people, many of whom watch for stupid gun handling mistakes.

Many veteran shooters insist that there is no such thing as a "gun accident." There is firearms negligence, which has often led to a tragedy. If one treats every firearm as though it were loaded—even if you have personal knowledge that it is not loaded—you will definitely be ahead of the curve.

Shooting negligence often is the result of poor storage practices and more often the result of poor gun handling skills and practices.

Don't leave a loaded firearm where a child might find it. If you're not using a firearm and instead are storing it, make sure it is unloaded...and then make sure again.

Split-second decisions, reactions

One thing about a violent encounter that is pretty common is the speed in which they unfold. Violence does not happen on a prearranged schedule and criminals do not call ahead to warn of their arrival. A violent crime usually happens fast, and the perpetrators are predators, while private citizens are their prey.

The dynamic that has changed in recent years is the increasing number of intended victims who are armed. No criminal hoping to live long enough to become a recidivist will just arbitrarily pick a target.

As reported in Chapter One about the axe-wielding man who attacked the store clerk and customer at a convenience store near Seattle, the whole incident lasted about 12 to 15 seconds.

Training and practicing—two different things, actually—are important when it comes to self-defense. One trains both mentally and physically, while practicing shooting and improving one's marksmanship skills raises the odds that you're going to hit that at which you are shooting, because a bullet that misses the target will hit something else.

Confidence in one's skills and one's firearm is part of that mindset formula. This can only come with experience and practice.

Ayoob has suggested that people hoping to keep their skills honed might consider participating in local gun club shooting competitions, so-called "action pistol" matches against which one matches his or her skills with a time clock. Racing against a clock does sharpen one's reflexes, and that could come in handy in the event of an actual life-threatening situation.

And that brings us around to a term that one will see in magazine articles and hear during any advanced course on pistol craft: "situational awareness." This kicks in when one enters Cooper's Condition Yellow, Orange or Red. Pay attention to what is going on around you and act, or react, accordingly.

The decision to engage in a self-defense action is overwhelmingly reached in a matter of seconds, if not split seconds. This is not an action that occurs in the same way it does on television or in a motion picture, and you will not have the benefit of hindsight, but investigators and prosecutors will.

If you attend an advanced training course, you will likely hear this more than once.

Try different courses

Thanks to the availability of different firearms "schools" there is an array of courses, from basic to advanced level. Many people who are seriously involved in training will attend different courses offered by the different schools in order to absorb as much practical information as possible.

One should never try different courses in order to compare and make a subjective determination about which is better than the others. Instead, the goal here is to learn new and different things, gaining as much knowledge and insight as is humanly possible for the purpose of surviving a gun battle should the unfortunate encounter happen.

This might be the best way to describe true "common sense gun safety" because the armed citizen will be learning from more than one source. If variety is the "spice of life," then one will find ample amounts of "spice" by attending courses offered at the different training academies.

One can find advertisements for such training in popular firearms periodicals or online. Just use your favorite search engine to find "firearms training" and you will come up with several options.

Some people might go to Gunsite in Arizona, Thunder Ranch in Oregon, Frontsight in Nevada, the Firearms Academy of Seattle in Washington, or some other facility that teaches defensive shooting skills and tactics. Or, they just might attend a course at all of them.

These are not places where people travel to learn how to kill. These are places where lawfully armed citizens travel to learn *how not to be killed*, and how to survive an armed encounter.

There are several such "shooting schools:" around the country, and one can find videos online from some self-styled "trainers" that suggest their courses should be avoided. After all, one does not wear the same clothing, or eat the same food, day after day without getting locked into a pattern.

The good academies all have references, and reputations to protect, so they're not going to promoting bizarre skills. You will be able to tell why by arriving on the premises.

Reputable firearms training facilities will invariably stress the importance of continued practice, firearms maintenance and above all safety. Many armed citizens will practice much more than some sworn law enforcement officers, who may quality twice a year. Those practice sessions could one day be a factor in saving your own life, or the life of another person.

The best place to begin such a training experience may be at your local gun range, or by checking with a gun shop in your area about the proximity and availability of firearms safety courses, usually taught by NRA-Certified firearms instructors. Such courses are reasonable in cost and time, and they will at the very least provide the experience to step up to the next level of training, which may be to attend one of the aforementioned shooting academies.

Be sure to have good eye and ear protection, and be willing to invest in quality gear, such as electronic hearing protection, often called "muffs." You only have one set of eardrums and eyeballs. One might even keep a spare set of "eyes and ears" in one's vehicle.

Use quality commercial ammunition for your training, and for personal protection. Virtually all of the major ammunition manufacturers offers loads in the popular calibers — .32 ACP, .380 ACP, 9mm, .40 S&W, .10mm Auto and .45 ACP — for personal protection.

Document your training

Whatever else one accomplishes at a good shooting academy, one can document when he or she took the course. In the event that you ever are involved in a lethal confrontation, that information could become valuable for your defense, should you ever be charged with a crime relating to the use of force in self-defense.

Ayoob's *In The Gravest Extreme* goes into this eventuality in considerable detail. Even today, the book is a useful reference for the armed citizen.

For the person who attends such courses, keeping a log of all of these is a good idea even if you are never faced with prosecution for acting in self-defense. If nothing else, the training one receives can be a useful tool during a debate with someone devoted to public disarmament who argues that private citizens are careless, untrained and unable to act in a self-defense emergency.

Some people go so far as to log each time they visit a gun range, and even keep track of the rounds they fire. Proficiency has its own reward, a fact that can make the difference if, or when, the unthinkable happens.

No matter how much one learns, one can always learn something more.

10: SOME INCONVENIENT TRUTHS

Following the 2018 tragic mass shooting of students and adults at Marjory Stoneman Douglas High School in Parkland, Fla. mentioned previously, there was much debate over the role of firearms in society, and whether private citizens should be allowed to own so-called "assault weapons" and "high-capacity magazines."

There was also considerable debate over the notion of allowing armed teachers in public schools, and a commission established to investigate the Feb. 14 tragedy that claimed 17 lives even suggested allowing volunteer teachers to bring firearms on campus. That idea was immediately criticized by ivory tower legislators and educators, and liberal pundits.

To the extremists determined to inflame public hysteria, no amount of gun control would be enough. Their goal is not to control guns but to be rid of them altogether.

In the midst of this discussion, co-authors John Malcolm, vice president of the Institute for Constitutional Government, and Amy Swearer, visiting legal fellow at the Meese Center for Legal and Judicial Studies, wrote an opinion piece that might be considered blasphemous by the gun ban crowd.

Their essay was headlined "Here Are 8 Stubborn Facts on Gun Violence in America." The list is rather simple:

> • Violent crime is down and has been on the decline for decades.

- The principal public safety concerns with respect to guns are suicides and illegally owned handguns, not mass shootings.

- A small number of factors significantly increase the likelihood that a person will be a victim of a gun-related homicide.

- Gun-related murders are carried out by a predictable pool of people.

- Higher rates of gun ownership are not associated with higher rates of violent crime.

- There is no clear relationship between strict gun control legislation and homicide or violent crime rates.

- Legally owned firearms are used for lawful purposes much more often than they are used to commit crimes or suicide.

- Concealed carry permit holders are not the problem, but they may be part of the solution.

The last three "stubborn facts" are met with equally stubborn resistance from gun prohibitionists, for they dare not accept, much less agree with, their unshakable notions—regardless of their flimsy foundations—that all guns are bad, and all gun people are simply criminals waiting to blossom.

But there can be no argument that inner-city body counts are, more often than not, the product of a hard-core criminal element. The number of people arrested in connection with murders committed in the United States who have prior arrests and convictions for any number of crimes might be staggering to some because they will wonder just how it is that individuals with such criminal and often violent pasts can still be free on the street, committing more crimes.

Even in the cases of mass shooters, many of these individuals have given off so many proverbial "warning signs" that when the shooting stops and the press goes to work, digging up all sorts of facts, their readers are often first to ask, "Why wasn't this guy in jail or a mental hospital?"

Mass shootings are almost invariably followed by emotions including grief, anger and finding blame. Too often, thanks to well-funded efforts, public anger is channeled toward the so-called "gun lobby," which actually consists of millions of law-abiding citizens who vote, own guns and often provide financial support to their favorite Second Amendment rights organization.

Then the blame game begins, with finger pointing toward firearms rights groups, which are more numerous than some might imagine. The leading national gun rights organizations include the Second Amendment Foundation, Citizens Committee for the Right to Keep and Bear Arms, National Rifle Association and Gun Owners of America.

They are joined by regional organizations that may have full-time lobbyists on staff, but usually rely on the activities of seasoned volunteers.

Still, even with capable staffers who know their stuff about gun use in crime and violence, it remains one of the more frustrating facts of modern American life that local politicians, especially mayors and city council members, resort to calling the gun owners names, and demanding ever-restrictive gun control laws that are uniformly ineffective and might even be unconstitutional. That can only be determined through court challenges, and they're getting increasingly expensive.

Bad guys with guns

Perhaps nothing better illustrates the abject failure of anti-gun politicians to realize and acknowledge the failures of their own policies than the past few years in Seattle, Washington.

Once celebrated as the "Jet City" for being home to the Boeing company, in recent years following a string of elections that placed increasingly left-leaning politicians in the mayor's office and on the city council, Seattle became something far less desirable. One local broadcast journalist did a special report headlined "Seattle is Dying" that received rave reviews from the public, but anger and denial from city officials.

For its size and population, Seattle has a remarkably low number of homicides. The city is surrounded and encompassed by King County, where monthly reports from the state Department of Licensing reveal about one in five state residents licensed to carry concealed handguns live.

But as Malcolm and Swearer revealed in their report, the higher rates of gun ownership do not have a direct link to crime rates.

Seattle is a special case. In 2015, the city council under then-Mayor Ed Murray, a perennial anti-gunner who unsuccessfully tried to push gun control legislation during his time in the State Senate, adopted a "gun violence tax." Proceeds from this special tax were predicted to add between $300,000 and $500,000 to the city coffers, which would then be used to study "gun violence" and prevent it through education and intervention.

But the tax drove one gun store out of the city and another to send its customers to a branch store in a neighboring county. The first full year of revenue came in at $103,766.22. The following year saw the city pull in $93,220.74. During its third year, the score was even lower, with only $77,518 reported.

Gun owners simply went outside the city to purchase firearms and ammunition.

And what happened to the homicide rates? In 2016, the city reported only 18 slayings. The following year saw the number climb to 28 murders. Three years out from adopting the tax, there were 32 slayings in the city. So much for the effectiveness of the gun control tax.

There is more to the puzzle. According to Malcolm and Swearer, the Brady gun control lobbying group "ironically makes this clear with its ratings for states based on gun laws."

"'Gun freedom' states that score poorly, like New Hampshire, Vermont, Idaho, and Oregon, have some of the lowest homicide rates," they wrote. "Conversely, 'gun-control-loving' states that received high scores, like Maryland and Illinois, experience some of the nation's highest homicide rates."

When there was a very high-profile holiday weekend shooting in the parking area at a popular Seattle park, Mayor Jenny Durkan acknowledged to reporters that during the previous months, there had been "a number of shootings" in the city's central district. These incidents were spilling over into neighboring jurisdictions.

"We believe, as the police have indicated, that there is a number of rival gangs that are having some turf issues," she admitted.

Gang members do not bother with concealed pistol licenses, nor are they typically legal gun owners. Teens cannot legally carry concealed handguns, anyway, in the state, especially if they have criminal records. Still, their dangerous feuding feeds demands for additional gun controls on law-abiding citizens who are not creating the problems.

When a rookie female police officer in Sacramento, Calif., was fatally shot, the accused killer turned out to be something less than a model citizen. The suspect had been involved in what the *New York Daily News* described as "a series of criminal cases dating back as far as 1995 – including several domestic violence and battery cases as well theft and driving under the influence."

Yet the suspect in this case reportedly had firearms in his residence, including some that are illegal under California statute.

Individuals with that kind of record are not permitted by law to possess, much less legally own firearms. Indeed, a frustrated public wonders how such people are even free on the streets to cause more mayhem when they should still be in prison doing time for crimes for which they were already convicted.

Farther south, police in Culver City responded to a shooting only to wind up in a lengthy stand-off with the suspect, who ultimately took his own life in a motel room. The suspect had shot another man in the neck, but he survived that bullet wound.

It turned out that the suspected gunman was a parolee with a history of violent crime including assault with a deadly weapon, according to KTLA News. Under federal and state law, people on parole are not allowed to have firearms.

Back in Illinois, a man who opened fire on U.S. Marshals in a Rockford hotel was identified as having a "long criminal history" in the state dating back to the 1990s. This individual had been convicted of domestic battery, criminal trespass, reckless discharge of a firearm, possession of a firearm by a felon and a list of other offenses, according to a local NBC affiliate.

Or take the case of Ruben Houston III of Wausau, Wis. According to the Appleton Post-Crescent, this individual had a criminal history that included more than one incident of being a felon in possession of a firearm. But that record came to an end in Appleton, where Houston died in a gunfight with local police.

His misadventures with the law dated back to 1990 and included illegal gun possession, drug possession, and assorted other felonies. He drew a six-year prison sentence in October 2002 for possessing an unregistered firearm and a month later, he was popped for possession of a firearm by a felon.

Meanwhile, in Washington State, some 200 miles from Seattle, a Vancouver man suspected in the slaying of a woman during an armed robbery was only 19 years old at the time, but his criminal history is an eye-opener. He was arrested for robbery at age 14, according to the *Longview Daily News*. His juvenile record included assault, burglary and theft, but he graduated to first-degree murder.

The list of bad guys with guns is almost endless, but they all have a few things in common. Gun control laws that impair the rights of law-abiding citizens didn't keep them from getting guns, and laws against felons having firearms didn't even slow them down.

They don't buy guns at gun stores or gun shows. Yet they seem able to get firearms when honest citizens are stuck with background checks and waiting periods, and maybe other red tape depending upon the jurisdiction and local gun laws.

When a man identified as Deshawn Brim of Raytown, Mo., was fatally shot while allegedly attempting an armed robbery of a cell phone store in Overland Park, Kansas, he was on parole, according to information posted on the website of the Missouri Department of Corrections.

His fatal mistake was in attempting to rob a store in which the manger/clerk was also armed. Published reports from the *Kansas City Star* and *Shawnee Mission Post* said Brim entered the store, brandished a gun and demanded cell phones. He reportedly jumped over the counter, giving time for the clerk to draw his own gun and fire. The 35-year-old robbery suspect died right there from his wound.

Gas station convenience stores are a "convenient" target for armed robbery. When a would-be armed robber tried to stick up one such business in Mount Clemens, Mich., one summer afternoon, he discovered the hard way that clerks can have guns, too. Wearing a mask, the robber tried to not only rob the store but also its customers.

The clerk drew his own legally-carried handgun and shot the 27-year-old suspect, who was transported to the hospital.

According to the Fox News affiliate in Detroit, the suspect in this caper was also a "possible suspect" in "other, similar crimes."

The clerk had the criminal out-gunned, too. The clerk was carrying a 9mm pistol while the perforated bad guy was reportedly armed with a .22-caliber revolver.

But there is a link...

While there may be no link between private gun ownership or the number of concealed carry licenses or permits and crime, a stunning report from researchers at NYU showed "a causal link between print news media coverage of U.S. gun control policy in the wake of mass shooting events and increases in firearm acquisition."

This was almost certain to get two reactions from the mainstream press: ridicule or absolute silence.

Headlined "Mathematics Ties Media Coverage of Gun Control to Upticks in Gun Purchases," the study was led by NYU researchers in the Tandon School of Engineering "in collaboration with faculty at the UCLA Fielding School of Public Health and Northeastern University."

What the study revealed hardly seems surprising to anyone who has been around the gun rights movement for any length of time. When the press pounces on a story about so-called "gun violence" and the typical reaction of anti-gunners to propose more gun control, Americans head to the gun stores. It's essentially the same reaction one sees from gun owners when Democrats start talking about new gun controls.

According to the NYU news release, "Increases in firearm purchases following mass shootings are well-observed phenomena, likely driven by concerns that these events could lead to more restrictive gun controls."

The NYU research reportedly analyzed 69 "mass shootings" in this country between January 1999 and December 2017. They looked at data on background checks conducted each month and news coverage in the *Washington Post* and *New York Times* that discussed gun control policies.

There were "pronounced" spikes in background checks in pro-rights states including Alabama, Arkansas, Florida, Idaho, Kansas, Ohio and Oregon.

By no great coincidence, the same reaction can be found among Americans whenever there is talk on Capitol Hill or in the White House about gun control. Alarmed citizens will almost reflexively open their wallets and head for the local gun store. That's been happening since Bill Clinton was in office.

There have been some positive benefits from all of this angst. More people have come to appreciate the Second Amendment as a fundamental right, and the increased gun and ammunition sales have been a boon to the Pittman-Robertson Federal Aid to Wildlife Restoration law that was passed in the 1930s. This fund raises money that is apportioned to state wildlife agencies for projects that benefit both game and non-game species. In the decades that it has been in existence, billions of dollars have been raised for this important fund.

This is one of the most "inconvenient truths" out there. Hunters and recreational shooters, people who own guns for self-defense; they all provide more financial support for wildlife than all of the anti-hunting and animal rights groups combined. Their money goes to actual wildlife related projects and provides a fairly substantial portion of operating funds for wildlife agencies.

The Pittman-Robertson special excise tax is a federal program. Unlike the so-called "gun violence taxes" in Cook County, Ill., and Seattle, Wash., the P-R program has actually accomplished considerable good.

Level Playing Field

Yet another subject that anti-gunners refrain from discussing, at least matter-of-factly and without hysterics or attempts to spin the conversation, is how the availability of firearms for personal protection has helped a growing number of women.

News reports are often filled with stories about women who have defended themselves from sexual assault or murder, and defended their children as well, thanks to the presence of a firearm.

Take the case of a woman in Harris County, Texas who was cleaning her home one afternoon when confronted by a man who broke into her house. According to the account at KRKT News, the woman "retrieved a pistol" and took refuge in a closet.

But she didn't manage to hide forever, and when the intruder, who happened to be armed, open the closet door and confronted her, the unidentified woman opened fire.

In the aftermath, Harris County Sheriff Ed Gonzalez praised the woman for her actions.

"She was shaken up," the sheriff said, "but kudos to her. She could have been a victim. There's no way to know what could have happened. We're glad that she is alive."

It turned out that the woman had been burglarized in the past.

According to the online *Women & Guns* magazine, women have become more active in the political process, advocating for gun ownership and against restrictive gun laws that would prevent them from being armed for personal protection.

Some 50 women participated in an effort called "The DC Project" in which they traveled to the nation's capital and met with lawmakers over a four-day period. The campaign is described as "a nonpartisan initiative to bring 50 women, one from each state, to Washington to dispel common myths and garner support for gun rights. The project is the brainchild of Dianna Muller, retired law enforcement officer turned professional 3-gun competitor, who just represented the USA in the IPSC World Shotgun match, where she brought home individual silver and team gold medals. In 2016 Muller met with her legislator and wanted to encourage other women to do the same, so she asked colleagues in the shooting community to join her."

This women's group has gone to Washington, D.C. annually, explaining to members of Congress that anti-gun-rights movements such as "Moms Demand Action" do not represent the views of all women.

Women make up the fastest-growing segment of the American shooting public, and they are engaged in all endeavors, from competition to hunting. They participate in pistol leagues, attend some of the nation 's top flight shooting schools for advanced instruction, have become instructors, and are active in their home states lobbying on behalf of Second Amendment rights.

The National Shooting Sports Foundation closely watches trends in the marketplace and they did a study that revealed more than 74 percent of firearms retailers have seen a significant upswing in the number of female customers.

Many times women feel compelled to provide for their own protection, and their children, because of stories like the one out of Jacksonville, Fla. that involved the fatal shooting of a 24-year-old man against whom the woman who shot him had taken out a protection order. Unlike the story discussed earlier about Carol Bowne in Berlin Township, N.J. this time the woman was armed. Florida gun laws are far more accommodating to the private citizen; designed not to discourage or prevent lawful gun ownership, but to allow it.

According to reports carried by WJXT, the man was identified as Brandon Johnson, and he had been arrested months earlier on charges of domestic battery, discharging a firearm in public and drug possession. The woman, with whom he had two children, had broken up with him about three months before the fatal encounter. The woman had taken out a restraining order because he had allegedly physically assaulted and threatened to kill her.

Perhaps as a testament to the failure of protection orders to actually protect anyone, Johnson allegedly broke into his ex's home and she was forced to fire.

Gun ownership up

During his first presidential debate in the race for the 2020 Democratic party nomination, former Vice President Joe Biden relied on his ability to get by with a political cliché when he should have been more direct with his remarks about gun control.

Biden told the audience, "If more guns made us safer, we would be the safest country on Earth."

But there is a flip side to that argument. If more guns made us *less* safe, America would truly have, as the gun prohibition lobby continually complains, an "epidemic of gun violence." Gun ownership has climbed in the past decade, and some sources have suggested that a fair number of new gun owners are being secretive about it for an assortment of reasons.

However, as noted earlier in this book, a look at the FBI Uniform Crime Report shows that the number of firearm-related slayings in the United States represents a tiny fraction of all the people who legally own guns. Do the math. By some estimates there are more than 100 million gun owners in the U.S. and they own by some estimates as many as 300-plus million firearms of all kinds.

Against that figure, the FBI crime reports over the past several years shows that fewer than 12,000 people are murdered annually with firearms. Balanced against all the honest citizens who own guns and have harmed nobody, by perspective the number of slayings amounts to something of a fly speck.

This is not to say that a murder is not a tragedy. But there are estimates that as many as a half-million to more than 2 million times a year firearms are used in self-defense, and the overwhelming majority of those incidents do not involve shots fired.

Good guys with guns are also a rather peaceful lot, because they are not running around firing shots at people unjustifiably, as they are sometimes portrayed in the media.

However, as this and previous chapters have detailed, those good guys occasionally must press the trigger.

The Ultimate Inconvenient Truth

Quite possibly the most inconvenient truth about the actions and activities of legally-armed citizens may be found in Washington State. In a state where recent history suggests everyone votes for liberal Democrats who believe in gun control, one in ten adults is licensed to carry, and that figure has been rising each month for the past several years.

More than 600,000 adults have concealed pistol licenses in the Evergreen State, a fact that causes the gun control lobby no small amount of consternation.

Yet, while the state has adopted strict gun control laws by citizen initiative in recent years, the promise of those measures to reduce crime have been empty. Homicide is up, and it's not the legally-licensed citizens who are committing the crimes.

In 2014, a "universal background check" measure that was pushed forward with a $10.2 million campaign which said it would make the state safer. In 2014, according to FBI data, Washington reported 172 slayings, of which 94 involved firearms.

The following year, that number jumped to 209 homicides, of which 141 involved guns. In 2016, the number slumped off a bit, with 195 killings including 127 committed with firearms, and in 2017—the most recent year for which data is available, and three years out from passage of the gun control measure— Washington logged 228 homicides, of which 134 involved guns.

Regardless how one does the math, that doesn't look like a safer community has emerged, and cannot possibly be interpreted that way.

Earlier in this chapter, we discussed the homicide statistics just in the city of Seattle, where the state's gun prohibition lobby is headquartered. What all of this data reveals—and what the gun control lobby stubbornly refuses to even acknowledge—is that their strategies have failed to the point of accomplishing what some people say is "less than nothing." Using the Washington State experience as something of a microcosm of what has happened nationally, it might be fair to suggest that gun control proponents started off wrong and have stayed there ever since because instead of focusing on the perpetrator of a crime, they focused on the instrument.

The more gun prohibitionists push to suppress lawful gun ownership, and the exercise of the constitutionally-protected right to keep and bear arms, the more people will resist. Tell the American public they can't have something, and they are going to demand it.

The proverbial bottom line here is that gun control laws do not appear to have had the desired effect, and they evidently have had the opposite intended effect, which results in the decision reached by increasing numbers of honest citizens to take responsibility for their own safety. Thus, one sees a steady upswing in concealed carry, because the fact remains that people want to feel safe, and they want the ability to fight back if the necessity arises, and the tools that make such a fight possible.

And that, in a nutshell, is why we are witnessing an upsurge in the number of good guys with guns.

11: IT'S NOT A POPULARITY CONTEST

Constitutionally enumerated fundamental rights must never be subjected to a popularity contest, which is exactly what happens when anybody puts a gun-related measure on the ballot for a public vote.

Rights are sacrosanct. If one can be nullified by a popular vote, so can another, and another, until all rights guaranteed in the Constitution have been reduced to the level of regulated privileges. Once a people votes away its rights, those rights will be difficult, if not impossible, to restore. This is why law-abiding Second Amendment advocates and activists—not merely "supporters" who always find a way to insert the word "but" into their affection for the right to keep and bear arms—must remain constantly vigilant.

An interesting story in the *Wall Street Journal* that discussed New York City's attempts to avoid a U.S. Supreme Court ruling on the city's draconian handgun law said a lot about the dishonesty of the anti-gun mindset.

For generations, gun control laws in New York City and elsewhere have become incrementally more restrictive, but the people pushing those laws got away with their erosion of Second Amendment rights because the people against whom those regulations and laws were used essentially were powerless to fight, whether it was due to lack of funding, or reluctance of attorneys to take their cases. However, since the 2008 *Heller* and 2010 *McDonald* rulings by the Supreme

Court, along with several pro-rights lower court decisions, that scenario appears to be changing.

Still, there will always be someone out there, lurking in the shadows or brazen enough to jump in front of the nearest microphone and television camera, who will want to whittle away at your rights.

These are the people who are "okay" with someone in the neighborhood owning a shotgun or rifle for hunting, but really feel uncomfortable with the notion of an armed neighbor being willing to defend himself and his family, and maybe even his squeamish neighbors and their families in a dire emergency.

They are the people who contend that since it is okay to license drivers and register their cars, it should be equally acceptable to license gun owners and register their firearms. In short, they confuse rights with privileges, and cling to that erroneous perspective regardless of any historical and legal evidence to the contrary.

So the idea of submitting measures that invariably impair and infringe upon the rights of firearms owners, while accomplishing nothing in the effort to reduce violent crime and remove criminals from the streets, appeals to such people. Such schemes never actually work, but instead of admitting that, the gun prohibition movement instead argues that more erosion of the Second Amendment and similar protections in state constitutions is necessary for the desired outcome, which they will publicly insist is a crime-free environment, but privately they will admit they just don't like guns and wish to be rid of them. Without fail, the wrong people—law-abiding gun owners—wind up being penalized.

There was one paragraph in the *WSJ* article about New York City's gun control law that perpetuated something of a misunderstanding about the Second Amendment, or for that matter, any other amendment in the Bill of Rights. But it does somewhat explain why the gun prohibition mindset has taken hold. Here's what the *WSJ* report said:

"The Supreme Court last addressed gun-rights issues in 2008 and 2010, finding in a pair of landmark decisions that while the Second Amendment gives people the right to possess a handgun at home for self-defense, the government has regulatory power over firearms. Since then, lower courts have upheld most gun regulations."

The Second Amendment doesn't *give* anybody anything, and never has. Too many otherwise intelligent people simply don't grasp that. The entire Bill of Rights was adopted as a brake on government. It protects individual rights – natural rights recognized by the Founders to have existed long before the Constitution was written – and therefore must itself be protected zealously because it prevents government overreach.

Of all the individual rights protected by the Bill of Rights, the right to keep and bear arms has become perhaps the most controversial and as a result, the most unpopular among self-proclaimed "progressives" who believe their efforts to create a Utopian society are noble and above reproach. This is why gun control advocates can never acknowledge they are mistaken about their intentions, nor their means of accomplishing their disarmament goals.

The ends always justify the means, and admitting mistakes is not in their nature. This arrogant approach to the serious problem of violent crime invariably hurts the wrong people.

As noted in an editorial regarding gun control laws in California, the *Chico Enterprise-Record* had this observation: "We just wish more of these measures were focused on mental health, and keeping dangerous criminals off the streets in the first place, than targeting people who aren't doing anything wrong."

Returning momentarily to the comparison of licensing drivers to licensing gun owners, some unknown philosopher once popularly observed, "Gun control is like trying to reduce drunk driving by making it tougher for sober people to own cars."

What happens when it becomes tougher for honest citizens to legally own firearms? You get cases like that of New Jersey's Carol Bowne, murdered in her own driveway while waiting for the local police chief to approve her permit to purchase a firearm, as explained in an earlier chapter. Her case is a monument to the futility and fatality of strict gun control laws, because the man who killed her used a knife, which he obtained with no background check and not even any identification.

Allowing an infringement on any right via a public vote runs against the very grain of the constitutional protection of rights. A right is not a right at all if it is subject to the whim of an emotional electorate that might be guided by slick advertising campaigns and biased news reports.

Who Are the Good Guys?

This book has focused on the actions of legally-armed citizens; average people faced suddenly with extraordinary circumstances where choices are limited if they wish to remain alive. Good guys with guns come in all sizes and shapes, from all racial, ethnic, professional and gender backgrounds. It's not what someone may look like on the outside, but what resides inside—in their hearts, minds and souls—that separates the good guys from the bad guys.

In a perfect world, there would be no bad guys. But this is not a perfect world, it is the real world, and there are bad guys. There are also good guys who will stand in their way.

The "good guy with a gun" might be a teacher or a doctor, an attorney or housewife. They are the people willing to risk it all to defend themselves and their loved ones from harm.

And there are more of them every day. They're out there, walking among us, going through their daily routines, prepared for an emergency they hope will never come. Occasionally, the emergency arises, and sometimes it has an amusing conclusion.

Just ask a man identified by Jacksonville, Fla., police as Christopher Raymond Hill. His day went from bad to decidedly worse when he tried to hijack a car at knife-point.

According to WHDH News, Hill reportedly robbed a Walmart liquor store in Jacksonville and then attempted to flee in an SUV. That was his first problem, because the vehicle wouldn't start.

He then allegedly turned his attention toward a car driven by Scott Reardean, trying to jack the car at knife-point. It was then that Hill got his first lesson in disparity of force. Faced with the knife, and having been slashed on the arms and legs, Reardean reached for the gun in his car and gave Hill a close look, at which point the knife-wielding would-be carjacker sprinted to another car parked at a Starbuck's drive through.

But the woman driver stepped out of her vehicle, opened the trunk and pulled out a gun, aiming it at the hapless outlaw. He ran a second time, only to be found later by police, huddled in the restroom of a nearby barber shop. Considering all of the circumstances, this bad guy was extremely lucky that the two "good guys with guns" he encountered had the self-control to not justifiably shoot him.

When a man armed with a knife reportedly attacked two Athens-Clarke County police officers, both lawmen—individuals normally considered good guys with guns—drew their sidearms. The suspect reportedly tried to take one officer's gun, as apparently confirmed by body cam video, and that's when one of the officers fired. The suspect, identified as Aaron Hong, died at the scene.

This was one of those situations where a bad guy brought a knife to a gunfight, and the good guys had him outnumbered.

Quick Dismissal

Anti-gunners typically disregard the actions of legally-armed, law-abiding citizens who act within the parameters of self-defense law with their legally-carried, lawfully-owned firearms. Those honest citizens invariably had to jump through several bureaucratic hoops to legally own a defensive firearm, and as noted earlier in this chapter, the gun prohibition lobby has labored to place as many roadblocks in their path as possible, because they simply object to the idea of an armed citizenry. Mounting public votes on proposed limits to gun ownership is the most recent tool used by anti-gunners. They have weaponized the wealth of anti-gun elitists to launch one campaign after another, using each effort as a learning tool for their next effort.

Instead, they focus on the tragedies to discourage gun ownership, as if to suggest that every gun is a tragedy waiting to happen, and every gun owner has only the worst motivation to exercise his or her constitutionally-enumerated rights.

However, there is one group that doesn't take armed private citizens so lightly. The National Association of Chiefs of Police conducts an annual survey of the nation's "top cops" and consistently when they ask members about gun policy, the results are interesting, if not stunning.

The annual survey has consistently shown results that gun prohibitionists do not care to see.

30th Annual National Survey Results

The following survey questions were posed by mail to Chiefs of Police and Sheriffs in the United States. It represents a broad cross section of professional command officers involving every state and every size department. The survey was conducted for the 30th consecutive year by the National Association of Chiefs of Police. (321)264-0911. www.nacoponline. org, policeinfo@aphf.org. Permission to reproduce in whole or part is granted if credit is given to the National Association of Chiefs of Police © 2018.

FIREARMS

	Yes%	No%	N/A%

Should any vetted citizen be able to purchase a firearm for sport or self-defense?

	Yes%	No%	N/A%
	88.58	7.68	3.73

Does your department support nationwide recognition of state issued concealed weapon permits?

	85.07	11.09	3.84

Can qualified, law-abiding armed citizens help law enforcement reduce violent criminal activity?

80.57		14.93	4.50

Does your department use reality based/active shooter training?

	80.35	19.21	0.44

Does your department sell confiscated firearms to help meet budget needs or cover budget shortfalls?

	17.23	81.67	1.10

Source: National Association of Chiefs of Police

NACOPS respondents are overwhelmingly supportive of legally-armed citizens, and the strong support for allowing licensed citizens to carry across state lines is eye-opening. When 85 percent of any group supports something, that's a philosophical landslide.

Equally as important, more than 80 percent of these lawmen believe that law-abiding armed citizens help law enforcement reduce violent criminal activity. As previous chapters have certainly illustrated, armed citizens have taken a number of violent people out of circulation, which is invariably a help to law enforcement, and in the cases detailed in Chapter Four, at times armed citizens have come to the rescue of police officers and sheriff's deputies who are in danger of grave bodily harm or death. Such acts can never be over-emphasized.

Rank-and-file law enforcement professionals are typically supportive of armed citizens and the Second Amendment. One prime example has been found in Washington State where law enforcement organizations have taken strong positions against gun control initiatives passed there in recent years.

These are the people who will be expected to enforce any new gun laws, and many sheriffs—mindful of their oaths to uphold the Constitution—have been rather outspoken about the questionable constitutionality of some gun control measures. Perhaps not surprisingly, the establishment media tends also to ignore those lawmen and women when they take positions against gun control. Instead, they only seem to provide "headline" type coverage when cops support gun control, which newspapers traditionally support as well.

Occasionally a bright mind is able to cut through this foggy thinking, and when that happens, it might not provide an "epiphany moment" but it comes close. At the very least, providing hard facts where emotion generally rules can open some minds to alternative views.

Challenging the status quo has become a habit of Eugene Volokh, who teaches free speech and tort law and various other legal subjects at UCLA. He clerked for retired Supreme Court Justice Sandra Day O'Connor, and for former Judge Alex Kozinski at the U.S. Ninth Circuit Court of Appeals.

On one occasion, writing an Op-Ed for the *Washington Post*, Volokh noted that opponents of concealed carry scoff at the notion that an armed citizen might intervene in a mass shooting, and often challenge gun rights proponents to cite examples of cases where that has happened. Nobody should ever give Volokh an opening like that, because it's precisely what he did in a stunning essay detailing ten such incidents, including a couple that have been mentioned in this book.

While incidents involving armed intervention by private citizens in mass shootings may be relatively rare, so are mass shootings, themselves. Still, with growing numbers of "good guys with guns," the odds increase exponentially that more cases of mass shooting containment will occur.

Most incidents involving legally-armed private citizens are smaller crimes; everyday (unfortunately) occurrences in which a bad guy is suddenly confronted by a good guy who prevails. These do not always end in shootings. The overwhelming majority of such cases do not involve shots fired at all. This should hardly diminish their importance, for that is essentially what self-defense is really all about, rather than leaping into action against a madman.

The late Robert A. Heinlein, the extraordinary science fiction author, once remarked, "An armed society is a polite society. Manners are good when one may have to back up his acts with his life."

Typical armed private citizens are not looking for politeness so much as they are prepared to defend their lives against attack, and such attacks generally are mounted by savages to whom politeness is a sign of weakness. They are human predators; people who have had too many "second chances" from soft-headed judges.

As this book was being written, a man in Seattle, Washington with a criminal record dating back more than ten years to include some 22 arrests and 33 different court cases, had just been arrested for brutally attacking three older men in broad daylight on a downtown street. He stabbed them with a folding knife, a weapon he should not have had because a judge had ordered him not to have weapons when she reduced his sentence in an assault-related case to 45 days, including credit for 18 days already in custody.

By the time police located and arrested him, this individual had stripped naked and traveled several blocks from the crime scene. In the wake of the attack, for which there was no apparent motive, talk radio hosts mused that if an armed private citizen had intervened and shot this man dead in his tracks, authorities in liberal Seattle would have tried every strategy to prosecute that Samaritan.

Maybe, but perhaps not, because Washington has a very strong use-of-force self-defense statute.

But this case illustrates what the "good guys with guns" are really up against, and underscores why there are good guys with guns in the first place.

We do not live in an ideal world. We live in the real one, where there are career criminals on the streets like this man in Seattle. They are there because of weak laws enforced by weak judges who have the benefit of 20/20 hindsight, but rarely the experience of someone who has had to make a split-second life-or-death decision.

Legally-armed private citizens make such decisions every day, more often than not without firing a shot. These legally-armed law-abiding private citizens carry a huge responsibility, from which they do not shrink. They are often the proverbial "first responders," and on occasion, the proverbial "last man standing."

Their ranks are swelling, even as individuals and organizations labor to disarm them and decry the constitutional right that guarantees their right to keep and bear arms.

They are your neighbors, friends, family members and in the final analysis, they may be all that stands between Heinlein's polite society and social chaos.

They are the Good Guys with Guns.